AF228053

DAVID PUSTANSKY

Extreme Improv 2 Bigger Book of Improv Games by David Pustansky

Copyright © David Pustansky 2025

All rights reserved.

Published by Extreme Improv

www.xstreamed.tv

www.extremeimprov.co.uk

First published in 2025

extremeimprovcomedy@gmail.com

All artwork by David Pustansky

Paperback ISBN: 978-1-8381326-8-2

10 9 8 7 6 5 4 3 2 1

First Edition

JOIN THE EXTREME IMPROV COMMUNITY

Extreme Improv XStreamed welcomes you to join our continually growing community and get involved!

At Extreme Improv, we welcome performers from all over the world to take part in our projects. This includes Extreme Improv live or online shows, and the Geek Battle and Slam Jam Championship Wrestling shows.

XStreamed Website: www.xstreamed.tv

Extreme Improv Website: www.extremeimprov.co.uk

Support my content on Patreon: www.patreon.com/extremeimprov

Extreme Improv Social Media

Facebook: www.facebook.com/extremeimprov

YouTube: www.youtube.com/extremeimprov

X: www.x.com/extremeimprov

TikTok: www.tiktok.com/@extremeimprov

Instagram: www.instagram.com/extremeimprov

Twitch: www.twitch.tv/extremeimprov

Snapchat: www.snapchat.com/add/extremeimprov

Bluesky: www.bsky.app/profile/extremeimprov.bsky.social

Threads: www.threads.net/@extremeimprov

Myspace: www.myspace.com/xstreamed

Join our Facebook Group for Performers

www.facebook.com/groups/extremeimprovxstreamed/

Extreme Improv Online Shows

- Extreme Improv XStreamed
- Geek Battle
- Slam Jam Championship Wrestling Show
- Jesters Jam
- Geek Battle Gaming
- Jet Lagged and Loving It
- XStreamed Zone
- Revenge of the Werewolf
- Geek Battle Galactic

OTHER BOOKS FROM EXTREME IMPROV

Extreme Improv Big Book of Improv Games

Extreme Improv Ultimate Guide to Creating Virtual Theatre

Extreme Improv Improviser's Bucket List

Extreme Improv 2 Bigger Book of Improv Games

BOOKS COMING SOON

Extreme Improv 3 Super Book of Improv Games

From Brawl Out to Brawl In

Evolution of Video Games

Scratch (Playbook)

Table of Contents

I: INTRODUCTION

Welcome back! And if you're joining me for the first time…just welcome! This is Extreme Improv 2 Bigger Book of Improv Games! And this is a direct follow up, or sequel, and continuation to the original Extreme Improv Big Book of Improv Games that I wrote and published in 2020!

First, and foremost, I hope you find this book really useful. For you, for your improv team, or place of education, or wherever it is that you intend to play all the improv games included. For me this book has been a long time coming. It has been an almost five-year gap between the original book and this direct follow up.

You won't need to have read the original Extreme Improv Big Book of Improv Games for you to be able to dive in and enjoy all the improv games covered in this guide. However, I'd certainly recommend you get that as well as this, for two important reasons. The first of which is it'll help my sales, which obviously as the author I'd be pleased to see…

But the less self-serving reason I'd recommend you get the original book is because I cover a lot of games in that book that are more common within the world of improv and so provide a good foundation for everything I'll cover in this book.

Truthfully, work on this book began before the first book was completed, and in the four years since then, I've been continually making notes on ideas for new improv games. I've also made a list of some of my favourite classic improv games that I hadn't covered in the first book.

It's always been my intention to write a second book in this series, but along the way both life and other projects have taken priority. I have actually released two other books in the Extreme Improv series which include the Extreme Improv Ultimate Guide to Creating Virtual Theatre which released in 2022, and The Improvisers Bucket List which came out in 2023. But neither of those were a direct continuation of the guide to improv games.

Creating and developing new improv games has been a huge passion in my life. I love teaching improv to people brand new to the world of improvisation, and really love teaching new games to experienced performers.

By the middle of 2024, I decided that I needed to knuckle down and get working on this follow up. Even though I had occasionally sat down to start writing the meat and potatoes of the actual book itself, I knew that the book was going to take a dedicated effort to put together.

The biggest challenge to get this book done has been that I had jotted down ideas for what could be literally hundreds of new improv games. Of all the new ideas I've had in the last few years, I've developed many of these that have been played in Extreme Improv shows, and in rehearsals. But many of these weren't yet developed enough to unleash on the world in book form.

For several months I've sat down and tinkered with dozens and dozens of new games, new formats, and new twists on classic games. These have been played in rehearsals, and within Extreme Improv shows and workshops. I'm now at the point where I am confident enough that I can present them in this second volume of improv games, and think people are going to love playing the new games I've developed.

Creating new games has always been very important for me. I love the classic games but think one of the things that makes Extreme Improv special is that I'm always looking to do things that people haven't seen before.

The original book contained guides on how to play 104 short form improv games, and I think I'm being fair to say that I created around half of them. I'm always hesitant to absolutely hang my hat on any particular game creation, as I always say that two cavemen could have independently *'invented fire'* without knowing the other had discovered it.

So, even though I believe I invented games like the Impression Battle Royale, The Ancient Egyptian Hieroglyphics Game and Alliteration Anarchy, I know it's possible that other improvisers may have come up with similar concepts before me. It may just be that they're playing them in their local theatre in a random town in Norway or Canada, and the games may never see the light of day outside a small community.

That is another reason why I've come back with a second book of games. I do love inventing new improv games, and for me that creates a few problems.

I don't want the games I develop to be stuck in that small town no one has ever heard of. Nor do I want them to just fade away and be lost to time if and when the Extreme Improv XStreamed shows come to an end *(never planning that to happen by the way – we'll outlive Methuselah)*. Also, and more importantly for me, I really feel proud of some of my creations, and want to see them become standard games within the world of improvised theatre. I can't do that if I keep them close to my chest or exclusive for Extreme Improv.

The only way I'll be able to continue playing these new games, is if lots more people know how to play them. I'd also love for them to grow and inspire new games from others. I'd like to see other people learn them, tinker with them and evolve them further into new variations I could only wish I had thought of.

The last reason I've written this book now is because I've been bursting to share all my new improv game ideas with everyone! At the end of the weekly online Extreme Improv XStreamed shows, I'll usually give a plug to say that *'viewers can learn how to play all the games we've played on the show from the original book'*.

Well... as time has gone on, I've had to adapt that slightly to say *'most of the games'*. As time has gone on further, I have found myself not introducing new games into the shows because I've felt protective that I don't want to give away all my new ideas before they're fully developed, and before I can write about them in this second book. And that goes against my wanting Extreme Improv to always deliver something new.

Of the over 120 games in this book *(even more counting variations)*, I'd be bold enough to say that I have developed approaching 100 of them. That is a bold claim, as I'll be the first to say that you could whittle that number down if you exclude games that are variations of classic games that include my patented *'Extreme Twists'*.

For example, in the first book, I'd say I was the first to introduce the idea of a *Reverse Alphabet Scene* and *QWERTY Alphabet Scene*. However, these are both derived from the original, classic, and probably most accessible version of the game, the standard *Alphabet Scene*. And that is most certainly not something I'm taking credit for.

For whatever my contributions to the world of improv may be, I'm proud to say that I stand on the shoulders of giants. And I salute the forebearers that have spent decades laying the groundwork for improvised theatre that is loved by so many.

Some of the games covered in this book include improv classics like *The Dating Game, Old Job New Job, Irish Drinking Song* and *Weird Newscasters*. Like with my first book, I'm happy to give my insights into how to play these favourite games that performers have been playing across the world for decades.

Then there are the games which I have developed as new variations on classic formulas. Games I'm excited to share include joke telling games like *Doctor Doctor*, and *Stopped by the Copper, Rhyming Choices* and *Try Again*, both of the latter are inspired by the classic game *New Choice*, and *Mischaracterisation*, which is inspired by the classic game, *Here Comes Jack*, which itself is also included.

And then there are games *(which I believe)* are wholly new creations of mine. These include *Three in a Boat, Pun Panic, Midwife Crisis, The Evil Phonetic Alphabet Game, Threes a Crowd,* and *The Birds and the Bees*.

I've tried my best to include a large range of different types of games and there are ones that are language based, physical based, singing based, games based on memory and lots of joke telling formats.

If all goes to plan, I can promise you that the journey will not end with this book being the second and final volume. The truth is, one of the challenges I've faced is that I've had to split my work into what will eventually become at least volumes 3 and 4. I had hoped to go the route of famous films like Back to the Future, The Matrix, or Lord of the

Rings, and produce all the sequels in one foul swoop. However, as I originally intended this book to release in the fall of 2024, I could see that target would be missed. If I were to finish several volumes at once, it'd delay the release of volume 2 by even longer.

The good news is that if you're reading this, it means that *'Extreme Improv 2 Bigger Book of Improv Games'* is now in the hands of everyone to enjoy. Hopefully, me effectively announcing future volumes within this introduction won't jinx their future release, and they should be available a lot sooner than it took for this one to follow the first!

So, without further ado, you are once again about to enter the world of Extreme Improv...Good luck!

II: ABOUT THE AUTHOR

Hello! My name is David Pustansky, and I am an actor, director, teacher, content creator and I guess as this is my fourth published book, an author.

I am the creator of the Extreme Improv Comedy Show, and all of the connected and related shows from Xstreamed.tv such as Geek Battle, Jet Lagged and Loving It and the Slam Jam Championship Wrestling Show.

I like old comedies such as the Carry On films, and the Abbott and Costello movies...and to be honest, I'm not sure if that is the kind of thing I should include in an *about the author* section. I think it is probably somewhat relevant in a book about performing improv comedy, as at least you'll gain an understanding as to some of my comedy influences.

I trained as an actor at a London drama school, having graduated in 2011, and have worked in various areas of the performing arts and entertainment industry ever since. I've acted in films and on stage and love to create my own projects.

I love the challenge of creating things, even if they don't necessarily relate to my training as an actor. Some of the things I'm proud to have created include the books I've written as author, the *'Extreme Improv Improvise Your Way Outta This'* board game, the Extreme Improv and Flight of the Vampire Penguins apps, and I also make a pretty decent pasta bolognaise... I'm not sure I'm the best at making any of these things, but I do believe you should always keep trying.

I do a fair number of online shows, and these fall between the realms of podcasts and virtual theatre. I'd like to think that I've done a decent amount to help further the development of virtual theatre as a concept, and at the time of writing, I believe I've probably produced more virtual theatre shows than any other individual producer out there.

My favourite video game is Donkey Kong Country 2 on the Super Nintendo, and I'll be honest, I don't think this *'about me'* section sells me as well as I have done in my previous books.

I guess that is because I feel like a lot of what I have to say is just duplication. Not just because I have essentially said a lot of the same things in my previous books, but because a lot of what I do comes under the Extreme Improv name. Unless you want to hear about why I hate celery, or that I hold a pen differently to most other people, I should probably just move the book along to the next chapter. A lot of my most interesting work comes under the Extreme Improv banner, so let's get onto the *'about Extreme Improv'* section...

III: ABOUT EXTREME IMPROV

So, you'd like to know about Extreme Improv eh? You've come to the right chapter. Extreme Improv was created by me, David Pustansky, during the year 2010, whilst I was still at drama school.

Originally named The ImProDigies Theatre Company *(and yes, the name was stylised that way)* the company was eventually renamed to Sparky Buddy Productions when I didn't want it to focus solely on doing improv. It then kind of went full circle and is now known as Extreme Improv after our 2017 show Extreme Championship Improv. I shortened the name to Extreme Improv as it is more social media friendly.

There have been live in person Extreme Improv shows all over the UK, although we do most of our shows in London. The first Extreme Championship Improv show took place as part of the Camden Fringe Festival at the Camden Comedy Club, and it's at that venue where a large percentage of our live shows are held.

At the time of writing, we have a monthly in person show at the Camden Comedy Club on the second Thursday of every month. This usually features guest acts as well as the Extreme Improv Championship being on the line! So, yeah, come along and see the show if you're in town!

Extreme Improv has performed all around the world with performances in places like California, Alaska, Florida, and more places in the United States. It's also performed in Tokyo in Japan, and a bunch of places in Europe.

Extreme Improv do an awful lot of online content, and as I mentioned in the about me section, I'd like to think that Extreme Improv is a leader in terms of the world of virtual theatre. I'd created a podcast version of Extreme Improv in 2018, and I was able to quickly evolve this into our virtual theatre show that would connect performers from all over the world to perform improv together. I'd like to think in the early days of virtual improv, I was someone who helped work out what was possible and innovated with formats and presentation.

The weekly Extreme Improv XStreamed shows are approaching 600 episodes at the time of writing. We've also just had our fifth Extreme Improv XStreamed World Championship online festival to crown our 2025 World Champion.

This was the eighth virtual theatre festival produced by Extreme Improv XStreamed, and it's been a great way to connect so many from the worldwide improv and theatre communities.

I have been proud to see that many of the performers who originally met through online Extreme Improv shows have eventually connected and met up in real life. As Extreme Improv grows, I hope to see the community grow and connect more as a result. To date we've held three Extreme Improv UK Championship events live on stage, and there are plans for things to get bigger and better with each passing year.

A huge part of the expansion of Extreme Improv has been through the XStreamed part of the brand. *'XStreamed'* is a play on words that a lot of people don't understand until I explain it. For our first online show, I figured that since the word *'Extreme'* phonetically has the word *'stream'* in it, and our online show was being *live streamed*, people would understand that XStreamed was just a way to say Extreme Improv live streamed.

Most people didn't seem to get it, but I guess it's like how Pokémon is short for Pocket Monsters. Fun piece of trivia there if you didn't know that.

Well anyway, the XStreamed part of name allows me to sidestep the company away from the improv part of Extreme Improv at times. But why would I want to do that?

Well, one thing I discovered is that people found it odd if anything I did wasn't improv based. So XStreamed now acts as the connective tissue between Extreme Improv and our other related shows and brands like Geek Battle, Jet Lagged and Loving It, XStreamed Zone, and Slam Jam Championship Wrestling. XStreamed.tv is also the name of the website which acts as the hub for all of the brands, and this serves an important function for Extreme Improv's growth.

For me, XStreamed is all about fun and entertainment, and Extreme Improv is the heart of everything that is XStreamed. The only issue is that improv as an artform is still niche and misunderstood by many.

These other brands such as Geek Battle and Slam Jam heavily incorporate improv and improvisers and so act as a more accessible way for new people to discover Extreme Improv. Crafty I know. They also allow me to expand the scope and audience of Extreme Improv into themed live on stage Geek Battle and Slam Jam shows.

Developing where Extreme Improv XStreamed will go next is a process that takes a lot of planning and patience. This book is an example of a project that has been in the works for several years now. There are certain things that I have up my sleeve that I hope everyone will think is amazing when they launch. I also hope these new initiatives will skyrocket Extreme Improv to the next level, but doing things correctly unfortunately isn't the same as doing things quickly.

One thing I do know is the release of this book will unleash dozens of brand-new ideas for improv games that up to this point have only been played within the confines of Extreme Improv. Hopefully they will now make their mark on the world of improvised theatre!

Extreme Improv XStreamed is our long running virtual theatre show

IV: GETTING STARTED WITH IMPROV

Maybe you've seen improv on television, or you've been to see a show at your local theatre or comedy club. Whatever your introduction is, you've reached the point where you want to take the plunge and dabble in the world of improvised theatre yourself. That's excellent!

But now the question may be *'where to begin?'* Having this book is certainly a good step, as it'll give you a lot of tips and advice to thrive at the improv games it covers. Not only that, but an awful lot of the techniques across the book will be applicable to other games not covered, as well as other types of improv and as acting skills in general.

But...

Having this book will only take you so far on its own. To truly get started with improv, you are going to have to actually get started! And by that, I mean you'll need to find somewhere where you can try it.

There are lots of avenues into the world of improv, and how you approach it may depend on where you currently are in relation to improv and performing in general. But don't worry, even if you're not experienced as a performer, improv is one of the easiest aspects to get involved with and has one of the quickest paths to go from complete novice to being able to perform.

Some of you reading this will be completely new to the performing arts. Some of you may have done some performing either at a community level or professionally, and this may have been on stage or on screen. Wherever you are starting from, a good way to get involved in improv is through a class.

The traditional route has been to go to in person classes, but sometimes you may find that there aren't specific improv classes taking place in your area. If this is the case, you'll usually find that classes advertised as acting or drama classes will usually incorporate improvisation-based exercises as part of their programme.

These may or may not be focussed on improv enough for your wants/needs but are still worth considering. If there aren't specific improv classes in your local community, general drama classes can still be a good way to learn performing skills and stage craft, which will also help you to become a more capable improviser.

It's never been easier to find some classes in improv, as since the Covid-19 pandemic and the 2020 lockdowns, an awful lot of improv classes started online, and have continued online ever since.

Whether in person, or online, it's very easy to search for improv classes and opportunities on the internet. Social media platforms, like Facebook in particular, are a great source for these as there are many groups where you can find classes advertised or ask for advice.

If you're at the stage where you are about to start, or are just starting to take an improv class, the best advice I can give is to go with an open mind, and a *yes and* attitude.

The phrase *yes and* is the most well-known idea in improv and suggests that if you say *yes* to things you'll open up a lot more opportunities than you would if you said no, and block ideas. The *and* is there to show a willingness to not just accept ideas, but build upon them.

Of course, it would be over simplifying things to tell you to just say yes to everything. We'll get more into the 'yes and' concept in the book soon. My main point here is that when approaching a new class, go in with a willingness to learn.

Often people will approach improv feeling they need to show that they're already good at it. They may want to show off how funny or creative they can be straight away. It's great if you are naturally funny and creative, but something that will help you on your improv journey even more is showing a willingness to fail and be vulnerable.

Oftentimes people will approach improv, performing, and life in general on the backfoot. People are cautious to show vulnerability as it can be interpreted as weakness. Well, my dear reader, I'm about to present you with a cheat code for improv, and that is failure can be a bigger strength than success.

If you do something perfectly, that's great. Well done. But if you do something badly, but tried in earnest and gave it your all, people will appreciate your effort for trying. And there's a good chance that a joke that fell flat, a bad accent or poor impression will be funny because it has gone wrong. As long as they know you are improvising that is. And this aspect is key. Watching improv is a little like watching a daredevil attempt a stunt. Sometimes it goes wrong, but that is part of the entertainment.

I'll discuss this concept more throughout the book, but the only laugh you're guaranteed not to get is the one you didn't go for. If you do go for it, you risk failure, but you also risk success... and sometimes the biggest successes you can have come from perceived failure. As I said, you just have to start doing improv, and with every *'failure'* you are guaranteed to learn something. And sometimes that is *'YES that didn't go to plan AND next time I'll try it another way.'*

But let's say you are a bit more experienced, and you've come to this book because you've been taking your improv or drama classes, or you're already an actor, and now you want to take things to the next level. I hear you.

My advice to you would be to enquire to improv teams or schools if there are shows that you can get involved with. You may also find that companies are running auditions, and again the best way to find these would be through Facebook groups for improv in your area. Another route is casting websites. I'd only suggest joining the latter if you are more involved with the performing arts as improv opportunities are far from the majority on these sites.

If you're attending an improv audition, you may be tempted to show off that wit and creativity again. Once again that is fine if you want to do that, but I'd say there's a couple of other things to keep in mind also.

Show how good a listener you are in scenes.

Show off how well you endow other characters as well as yourself.

Show that you have a great personality and will be easy to work with.

And show that you are willing to learn.

Every improv group, teacher and director are likely to have their own style, and a great improviser will show how adaptable they are to different practices. If you usually approach things differently, be willing to try the methods that are present in the room you are actually in. There will certainly be time for you to introduce your own methods and skills the more involved you become.

If you're working with a good team, they'll all be willing to learn from one another. Everyone will be able to offer value if everyone is open minded.

And this brings me to the last idea I'll present to you about getting started in improv. What if you're at the stage where you would like to create your own improv group? This may just be so you can have fun sessions, or maybe you want to do shows.

Perhaps you're less experienced, but there really isn't a local source for in person improv. Fab, then see who you have in your community and work to create your own sessions, classes and shows.

Creating your own shows and groups is a big topic and one that goes outside of the scope of this book. I'll save that full discussion for the future, but I guess I'll give you this thought on the matter. Start small, do rehearsals and build trust and chemistry with your team. Work out what kinds of games or formats you'd like to do, and practice, practice, practice.

Improv can be for everyone. It is more accessible than ever with more in person opportunities and online shows and classes than ever before in history. If you want to get started in improv, there is no better time to start than right now! Where there is a will, there is a way, and you'll be amazed at what you can achieve if you approach things with that all important phrase *'Yes And'*.

V: SOME GENERAL TIPS

OK, so you're eager to start playing improv games and perform either on stage or online! Fabulous. Let's quickly go over some useful tips that will help you get the most out of your performances. These are some general tips on good practices to follow when doing improv with others.

#1: Accept offers from others and build upon them.

This is the famous *'yes and'* idea I was talking about during the *'Getting Started with Improv'* chapter. You'll hear certain terms and vocabulary in the world of improv and performing in general, and both *'yes and'* and *'offers'* are terms that are good to know.

For clarity, an *'offer'* is nothing to do with you getting offered a job or a placement on a course or anything like that. In improv, an *'offer'* refers to an idea or action that is presented to you whilst performing.

An offer can take the form of a character asking or telling your character to do something. It could also be a physical offer. This could be that another character offers their hand for you to dance, or it could be that they act like their holding something behind their back, or that they walk with a limp.

In all these cases, the choices made by another performer are offers, because they offer you an opportunity to acknowledge them, respond to them, and to go with and expand upon them.

If the character tells you to switch the light on, that was an opportunity for you to do that action. If the character limps, that is an opportunity for you to ask if they're ok.

If you go along with the offers and take the opportunities they present, the scene will create itself before you know it.

But you may think *'if I just do what the other performer gives me the opportunity to do, the other performer will always be in control and the 'leader'. Right?'*

No.

The phrase is *'Yes And'* but could be *'Accept and Expand'*. You go along with the offer and opportunity presented by the other performer, and that is saying *'Yes'*. But it is just as important that you say *'And'* and proceed to expand upon the idea and opportunity they gave.

For example:

Player 1: *Would you like to go bowling?*

Player 2: *Sure! And then we can play arcade games!*

This simple example shows how Player 1 presented an offer and then Player 2 accepts the offer and expands on it with an offer of their own.

#2: Avoid blocking and replacing

To build off the last example, let's look at two forms of blocking. Blocking refers to not accepting another performer's offer.

Player 1: *Would you like to go bowling?*

Player 2: *No.*

Now the above example may seem harmless enough, and there are certainly times where saying no is the right thing to do *(more on that in a minute)*. If, however, there's not a really good reason for Player 2 to have said no here, all they have done is stop the potential direction of the scene.

Either Player 1 will have to suggest an alternative activity for the characters to do instead of bowling, or the scene will become about Player 1 trying to convince Player 2 to go bowling. The option that will drive the story forward most quickly is just for Player 2 to agree to bowling. Then they can spend more time doing the bowling rather than just talking about the plan.

Another type of block can be seen in the following example:

Player 1: *Would you like to go bowling?*

Player 2: *Hey! I have an idea. Let's bake cookies!*

In this example, Player 2 didn't acknowledge the offer from Player 1 and just replaced the idea with their own. Either try to find a way where both ideas could be explored or don't worry about the scene being what you think it should have been. Ideally the scenes should be a collaboration, and no one player should block another's to get their own way. Doing that will quickly cause issues within your working relationship.

#3: Don't talk about the thing. Do the thing.

It can be easy for players to spend the whole scene talking about doing something rather than doing it.

If a character suggests going bowling, I'd aim for someone to be miming throwing a bowling ball within the next 20-30 seconds. If instead you spend the next several minutes debating if you should go bowling, or saying things like *I'm not good at bowling, where can we go bowling, what time do they open?, I'll need to buy bowling shoes* etc...that is all time you could have shown the audience what will happen when you actually do go bowling.

I'd suggest this rule is essential for short form improv. Most short form games probably last a couple of minutes, or five if you give them breathing room. That is too little time to spend the majority of the scene not doing the thing. If the audience suggest that the scene is about a werewolf, don't spend the whole scene waiting for the moon to rise.

Of course, there are exceptions to every rule, and the major exception on this front is 'long form improv'.

This book is focussed on short form improv games which are like sketches that play out in a short amount of time. As such, whatever you're going to do as the characters you play in a short form game need to be done in a condensed way. It is typical that you'll play different characters in every short form scene, so you really can't spend a long time developing the character and scenario.

In long form improv, which is most easily described as improvised plays, you'll be able to play the same character and scenario across several scenes. This means you have more opportunity for world building and to take your time over things.

Even with long form improv, I would still suggest you do the thing rather than talk about doing the thing. Don't let the longer running time of a long form piece just be consumed with filler. Don't talk about doing the thing, and actually do it...and let this lead on to whatever the next thing is. And do that too.

Whilst it's true that less can be more, it can also be that less is just less.

#4: Make sure you listen

Listening is one of the most important skills you'll need to develop to thrive as an improviser. And when it comes to improv, and performing in general, I always take '*listening*' as more of complex idea than just hearing what the other performers say. For me, listening is taking in everything else that is happening in your environment. It's hearing what others say and taking in it. It's seeing what others do and responding to what they do. I would say that this also extends to having awareness of your audience.

You'll often hear people in improv talk about '*listening more*'. At the heart of it, this message is to pay more attention. Pay attention to obvious things and also pay attention to fine details.

#5: Give the people what they want

Very simple this one. If the audience give you a suggestion, aim to deliver something that will satisfy their request. The audience want to see that what you create on stage is in response to what they suggested.

Again, this comes down to listening, but it's also about fulfilling promises. Improv shows are built around the idea that the performers are making something up on the spot. One of the reasons why its traditional to turn to the audience to ask for the opening suggestions is to prove that what you are doing is truly improvised and not pre-planned. If you disregard the audience suggestion, it'll let them down and also raise the question if what you did was truly improvised.

#6: Embrace failure

I've touched on this already, but it's worth reiterating. Lots of people who do improv are on the backfoot because they're nervous about doing *"something wrong"*. This can include the feeling of being judged for an action or dialogue choice, showing up that you aren't knowledgeable about something, or not performing a skill as you may like to.

For the most part, you really shouldn't worry about any of this. If the audience suggest that you play an opera singer and you know that you really can't sing at all…just try anyway. What's the worst that can happen? Everyone watching doesn't expect you to coincidentally be a great opera singer, and their expectation is that you probably will be bad.

Once again, give the people what they want.

If it turns out you are a great opera singer or can hold your own, you'll probably shock the audience and get a great reaction. If it turns out that you're not very good at it, you'll probably get a good laugh anyway for being a good sport and having a go.

If something goes great…great. If something goes, wrong…also great. Embrace going wrong and turn your weaknesses into strengths. As long as the audience see that you're giving it a go, they will be on your side. Once you understand this, you'll win even if things go wrong.

#7: Winning doesn't matter. Aim to entertain instead

Don't worry about winning at improv games.

I always say the aim of the show is to make it as fun and entertaining for the audience as possible. If you take the competitive side of the games too seriously, you're likely to restrict your creativity in the pursuit of following the rules down to the letter. This is less likely to project fun to the audience.

Winning is nice but shouldn't be anyone's main goal with the games. Concentrate on having fun with your scene partners and the audience.

Of course, this doesn't mean that you should act like you don't care about winning. Make it a character choice to act like you want to win but know it doesn't actually matter if you do win or not. It can be exciting for the audience if they think everyone is taking competitive games seriously, but this should just be to raise the stakes and enhance the experience for the audience.

It's worth having a discussion in rehearsals about competitive games and making sure everyone is on the same page and has the same values going into them. Even if you want the audience to think that the players are taking things seriously in competitive games, you should always aim to maintain a sense of teamwork and a supportive atmosphere.

#8: Use good stage craft

Whether you're performing on stage or online, you should always want to practice good stage craft. This means you should always take steps to ensure the audience can see and hear you as well as possible throughout the performances. This means:

not turning your back on the audience

making sure you project your voice

keeping your head up to be seen

avoiding standing directly in front of others to physically block them

and avoiding talking over other performers

#9: Reincorporation

A great skill you should develop for use in improvised theatre is the idea of reincorporation. This is where you say or do something that references something that was said or done earlier in the same show.

This may be repeating a joke, or referencing a line of dialogue, or reintroducing an idea or character from an earlier scene. Doing this will create a thread throughout the show for the audience to follow. Audiences are usually smart enough to pick up on repeated details, and the very fact that they recognise that an idea or joke has returned, can be enough to get a laugh or positive response out of them.

In comedy, they say there is a rule of three. You say a joke, and it may get a laugh. If you do a similar joke later, it can often get a bigger laugh than the first time. This is because you've now got a foundation that has been built upon. The rule of three idea suggests that doing it a third time, especially if done at a point where people may not be expecting it, can get a huge laugh.

The rule of three is an example of reincorporation. I will give the warning that it is a rule of '*three*', and if you attempt to keep revisiting a joke or idea too many times beyond three, you may start to get diminishing returns. This is what is known as '*milking it*'. This refers to milking a cow too much until the milk runs dry. If you push a joke onto an audience too many times you are likely to run out of comedic milk.

#10: Always treat others with respect

This one should be obvious, but it's always worth noting. Whether in rehearsals or during a performance, do make sure you treat others with respect. This includes other performers, theatre staff, directors, audience members etc.

I'd suggest that improv and theatre companies should have a code of conduct that you should make available for everyone. Make time to talk about what is and isn't acceptable behaviour during rehearsals.

VI: THE ROLE OF THE EMCEE

It is usual for a short form improv show to have some kind of Emcee or host.

The host will be the main go between the cast who play the games and audience who give suggestions. It is typical for the Emcee to do the following:

Introduce the show.

Introduce the improv games and challenges and explain their rules.

Ask the audience for suggestions and select the ones to use.

Start and end games and act as timekeeper.

Ask the audience to vote on any competitive games.

Who should be the Emcee?

Sometimes, the Emcee will not join in with the improv games and just be a person who acts as host throughout the show. Other times, a cast member will take on this role as well as performing in games. The Emcee doesn't have to just be one person either, and sometimes having two people work together like a double act can work well. Some groups have different members of the cast all take on the role of Emcee to introduce different games.

In Extreme Improv, I usually act as the Emcee for the shows, and I will also perform in the improv games. Sometimes this will mean I will ask a different cast member to introduce or Emcee a game that I am playing in.

Tips for the Emcee

#1: Practice introducing games

In this book, I've included suggestions of what the Emcee should say to introduce each of the games. This is just a suggestion, and you are free to explain the games in your own words. One challenge the Emcee has is that with each game there may be a new concept for the audience to take on board to get the most out of a game. Because of this you should aim for your introductions to be clear and concise.

#2: Make sure you understand all the games

The Emcee may or may not take part in any of the improv games. Whether you do or you don't, you should aim to understand how they all work. The Emcee can act as something of a referee and will often be the person to start and end games. If you don't understand how they all work this will be a lot more challenging to do.

#3: The Emcee has some power as director and editor

Some people believe you should take whatever the first suggestion is that the audience give you, but I'm slightly more relaxed on this idea. The Emcee is the person who will be asking for the suggestions, and has the power to select or decline any suggestions that do/don't work.

You shouldn't spend too long asking for suggestions and if you turn too many down, it will slow down proceedings for the show. This is where the Emcee can be considered something of a director and editor. If an audience member suggests a scene take place in a capybara pen at a zoo, and you feel this is too niche or limiting, the Emcee could say that they'll interpret the suggestion as being at a zoo. This will open up extra possibilities.

If an audience member suggests something that feels overdone or too bland like a *doctor's waiting room*, the Emcee has the power to ask the audience to build upon a suggestion and combine ideas. They could ask for something unusual that is happening at the waiting room or get another piece of information like who is a celebrity that is in the waiting room.

#4: The Emcee should be ready to save a scene or the cast.

The Emcee should really listen carefully during any scenes. This means paying attention to both what is happening in the scenes and paying attention to the audience. If it feels like a scene isn't working, the Emcee should look for openings to end the scene at the earliest opportunity.

There is a balance to this, because you don't want to end any game so early that the audience will know a scene has bombed, but you also don't want to leave performers in a scene for ages if they're struggling.

If a scene feels like it isn't working, you need to give the performers a chance to turn things around. If it isn't happening, let the scene play out the minimum amount of time needed for the audience not to suspect that you're just ending it, and look for an end point.

An end point could be after the audience give a laugh, or something dramatic has happened. You can bounce off these moments like they're cliffhangers.

If neither of these happen, I usually wait for a character to ask a question, and then as the Emcee, I will interject and answer it myself with something dramatic or silly. Either way, quickly move things on and encourage the audience to clap the performers who were just in the scene.

VII: HOW TO USE THIS GUIDE

OK, we're about to get into the list of games, but before we do, here is a brief rundown of how the games are explained throughout the book.

Below you will see an example of how the games are laid out in this book. You will see the various headings followed by an explanation of what information you will find in that section.

<u>EXAMPLE GAME NAME</u>

Emcee Intro Script: The Emcee Intro Script is an example script of what the Emcee could say to introduce each game.

In theory any performer should be able to understand enough about how to play each game simply from the rules being explained by the Emcee.

In practice, the Emcee's introduction of a game is designed primarily for the audience's benefit, and not the performers. To master most games there will be more rules and tips to follow than what the audience need to know.

For a performer to fully understand a game, please read the *How to Play the Game* sections which will give more details on how to play.

Challenge Style: This will explain the type of challenge each game is – scene based, monologue, song etc.

Players: This will explain how many players can play each game. This is just a guide and sometimes you may be able to adapt a game to use more or less players.

Ask the Audience For: This will give examples of what the Emcee should ask the audience for suggestions of *(sometimes known as 'gets')* so that the players have a starting point for their scenes. Feel free to use the examples given or come up with your own.

Setup: If there are special requirements needed for a game these will be listed here. This includes things like a chair, microphone or specific prop. If all you need is an empty stage and your imagination, the Setup heading may not be listed.

How to Play the Game: This section may seem like it's repeating information from the Emcee Intro Script, but that is not its intention. Whilst the Intro Script is there to explain the game rules to an audience, this section is there to give a detailed explanation of how a game works for the performers.

Some improv games have definite rules. Some have clear objectives. Many have steps to playing the game successfully which aren't quite correctly explained by either term. The rules and objectives in this section are broken down into numbered points, but please note that the points do not always have to be played in the order they are listed.

How Does the Game End? This section will explain how the game being played could be brought to a conclusion. This could be a judgement call made by the Emcee that the scene has reached a natural conclusion or run out of steam. It could be a time limit, an error made by a player causing them to be eliminated from the game, or a goal achieved by a player meaning the game ends with them winning.

Pro Tips: The Pro Tips section is to give some extra tricks of the trade to help you go from being a good player of a game to a great player of a game. Many of the tips from one game may be useful to be applied for other games as well.

See Also: This section will let you know if a similar game was also covered in a previous book in the series. Some games featured are new variations or closely connected to other games. You should be able to play any game featured in this book from the instructions given. I may recommend looking at another game already featured in the original Extreme Improv Big Book of Improv Games if there would be useful insights.

A note about rules, modifications and variations:

I have written that some games can be played with time limits, or with a certain number of lives, or played in teams. This is often optional, and can be played with or without these.

Games where I haven't listed these rules could still be played this way, and likewise games where I have listed teams or timers could be played without them.

As you practice games, play around with these elements and experiment with what works best for you. Modifying games can increase or decrease their challenge and I'd encourage you to be open to trying games tweaked in different ways as you may discover a new way to play that I've not listed.

VIII: THE LIST OF GAMES

Here we go again! For Extreme Improv 2 Bigger Book of Improv Games, this is the part you've all been waiting for...the games!

Over one hundred and twenty games await, so get ready to dive in and get inspired and try out all the new games that are now at your fingertips!

And...here...we...go!

The Extreme Improv Cuddly Koala gives you two thumbs up!

SECTION 1: GAMES FOR TWO PLAYERS

The first section of games are all games that are designed to be great for two players. These present a range of challenges for you to get your teeth into and are a great starting point to try out with a friend.

I've got your back!

1: LAST WORD FIRST WORD

Emcee Intro Script: This improv challenge is called Last Word First Word. Every time a player finishes a line of dialogue, the next player has to use the same word to start their next line of dialogue.

Challenge Style: Scene based

Players: 2

Ask the Audience For: An unlikely place to meet your boss

How to Play the Game:

#1: Either of the players can say the first line of dialogue, and they can start the scene by saying anything they want.

#2: After the initial line of dialogue has been said by one of the players, the second player will have to start their line of dialogue with the same word that ended the first player's line.

#3: This pattern continues for the entire game. Whatever word ends a line, has to be used as the first word of the next line.

For example:

Player 1: *How are you?*

Player 2: *You wouldn't believe me if I told you. It's bad.*

Player 1: *Bad luck. Sorry to hear that.*

Player 2: *That is kind of you to say...*

How Does the Game End?

This game can be ended by the Emcee when they feel it has reached a natural conclusion or run out of steam.

Pro Tips:

Pro Tip #1: Try to use the words in a different way to what the previous player did. It can be very easy to get into a pattern of the repeated word sounding like you're asking the other character a question. Either like you are surprised at what they said, or that you didn't hear them and want to confirm that was the word said. For example:

Player 1: *I have to tell you I'm pregnant.*

Player 2: *Pregnant? I knew you were hiding something from me.*

Player 1: *Me? Hide something from you? Never!*

Player 2: *Never? You hide things from me all the time.*

As you can see this will get quite samey. Try to mix things up between the two approaches shown in the examples given.

Pro Tip #2: The more confident you get with this game, the more you can challenge your scene partner by ending your lines with more interesting or challenging words. Whatever word you end with, will force them to have to start their line with the same word.

2: LAST LETTER

Emcee Intro Script: Our next game is called Last Letter. In this game each new line of dialogue will have to begin with a word that starts with the last letter of the last word of the previous player's line of dialogue. So, for example, if I said *'Hello, my name is Tom.'* The next player's line would have to start with a word that began with an *'M'* as Tom ended in a M.

Challenge Style: Scene based

Players: 2

Ask the Audience For: Something you would like to achieve.

How to Play the Game:

#1: Two players perform a scene where every new line of dialogue has to start with a word that begins with the final letter of the final word the previous player just said.

Here is an example, with the last letters highlighted to show how the game should work.

Player 1: *Oh my gosh, a snake has escapeD!*

Player 2: *Damn! They can be pretty dangerouS.*

Player 1: *Snakes are my biggest feaR!*

Player 2: *Rattle snakes are the worst oneS.*

How Does the Game End?

The scene ends at the judgement of the Emcee.

Pro Tips:

Pro Tip #1: Without going over the top, it's no bad thing to highlight the beginning letter of each new line of dialogue you say. By putting a little emphasis on some if not all of the words, it will help the audience understand the rules of the game and what you are trying to achieve.

Pro Tip #2: Whilst you are dictated what letter a new line of dialogue will begin with, you can choose any word that begins with that letter.

If you are able to start the lines with words that relate to the scene or are more interesting or complex words, you are more likely to impress your audience. But the priority should always be to make the scene make sense and keep the story going forwards. Don't hesitate whist you're trying to think of the perfect next word.

Z really is the last letter…

3: SECRET

Emcee Intro Script: Want to hear a secret? Me too, and luckily, Secret is also the next game we're going to play. In it, two performers will create a scene where one of them is hiding a secret. This secret will come to light within the first minute of the scene.

Challenge Style: Scene/Objective based

Players: 2

Ask the Audience For: A location where the secret is hidden. This could be in a box, on a phone, in a car, in a cupboard and things like this.

How to Play the Game:

#1: Two players should start the scene by establishing who their characters are, where they are, and how they know each other.

#2: After twenty to thirty seconds, the secret should be discovered by one player.

#3: What the secret is, and the reason for it, is something that is decided by the players during the course of the scene.

#4: The reveal of the secret can be handled in one of two ways:

A: The player who was keeping the secret is aware it has been discovered, and we instantly see the reaction of both players.

B: The player who discovers the secret finds something that shocks/surprises them and quickly conceals that they have found the secret.

#5: If you go down route A, from this point, the characters should discuss the secret and the reasons why it was kept secret.

If you go down route B, it means that the player who has discovered the secret can start to probe the other player about the secret. They can say things that will start to hint that the secret has been discovered.

If you go this route, you can actually get more out of the scene, as you'll now have more reveals.

The first reveal would be the player discovering the secret. The second would be the player who had the secret realising that their secret has been found out.

How Does the Game End?

The Emcee should end the scene once the secret has been revealed, and the players have had enough time to explore their reactions to this reveal.

Pro Tips:

Pro Tip #1: The player who discovers the secret should be the player to say out loud what the secret is. This way, there won't be any confusion of who gets to decide what the secret is, and both players won't get stuck passing the buck waiting for the other player to make a decision.

Pro Tip #2: Be clear as to what the secret is. If it's left vague, it'll be hard for the audience to follow.

4: MACGUFFIN

Emcee Intro Script: What's in the box?! We'll find out...maybe...as we play Macguffin! We will see a scene play out between two players where each player has a goal. During the course of the scene, one player will become interested to find out the contents of this briefcase/box *(this can either be real or mimed).* The other player will have to use every tactic they can to stop it being opened and the contents being revealed.

Challenge Style: Scene/Objective based

Players: 2

Ask the Audience For: A place where the scene takes place or a type of relationship between two people.

How to Play the Game:

#1: If you have a real briefcase/box, this should be one that can be opened and closed, and this should be positioned at the front of the stage. If it is being mimed, I would suggest that the Emcee still visually place it down as a point of reference for the audience and the players in the scene.

#2: The contents of the briefcase/box shouldn't be revealed at the start of the game. It should be saved as a reveal if and when it is eventually opened.

#3: One player should be very interested in opening the box, and the other player should not want it opened at all. You can decide who is wanting what before starting the game, or you can just figure it out as you go along.

#4: Of course, it would be very easy for the player wanting to open the briefcase/box to just pick it up and open it. Doing so would end the game quickly, so it needs to be an unspoken rule that the player whose goal it is to open it, won't just do so unless they have really explored the reasons to or not to open it.

The aim, as it should be with every game, is to make the scene entertaining for the audience rather than just to win. This means that the player who wants to open it has a slightly harder task than the player who doesn't want to open it. This is because the player who does want to open it will have to demonstrate that they want to open it, whilst allowing themselves to be prevented from doing so.

#5: The player who doesn't want the briefcase/box to be opened can use any tactic they want to stop it being opened. This should probably start with simple reasoning, and this can escalate as the game goes on. The longer the scene goes on, the more serious they should become in their tone and insisting that it isn't opened.

#6: Eventually, it can come down to the players physically trying to grab the briefcase/box and open or prevent it from being opened. This is something you should build up to.

How Does the Game End?

The game should end with it eventually being opened. You have the option to say/show what is in the briefcase/box or leave it as a mystery.

Pro Tips:

Pro Tip #1: If you are going with a briefcase rather than a box, you can play with the idea of it needing a key or combination to open.

Pro Tip #2: Avoid instantly making the scene about opening the box. Give yourselves a chance to establish the characters and relationship before your attention turns more and more to the box.

Pro Tip #3: If the focus has been on opening the box, it could build up to a crescendo, only for things to die down. The characters could then get on with other things whilst their interest in the box builds up again.

Pro Tip #4: You have the option to flip things around and have the characters switch who does and doesn't want to open the box. The way to do this is to have the character who doesn't want to open it be successful in convincing the other not to. Once things die down, the character who said not to open it should betray their own reasoning and decide they are interested to know what is inside.

5: YOU KNOW HOW I KNOW

Emcee Intro Script: Our next game is called 'You Know How I Know?' Two players stand opposite one another and have a revealing conversation. Audience, you'll suggest an opening idea that one of the players knows about the other, and they'll take it from there.

Challenge Style: Conversation/Scene based

Players: 2

Ask the Audience For: An opening suggestion of what one player will say they know about the other. For example that one player hates tennis, or that they killed the school rabbit, or that they have a crush on someone.

How to Play the Game:

#1: Two players face each other. We'll refer to them as Player 1 and Player 2.

#2: Player 1 starts the conversation with the opening line *'You know, how I know BLANK?'* The blank being filled in with the audience suggestion. Player 1 will then proceed to give their justification for why they know this about the Player 2. For example:

Player 1: *You know how I know that you have a crush on the gym teacher? You always turn red like you've run a marathon whenever he's around.*

#3: Player 2 is now free to respond to Player 1's assertion about them. Player 2 can either accept, explain or deny what Player 1 said they know about them. This can continue back and forth as a conversation between the two.

#4: At a certain point *(that is up to the players)* either player can make more assertions of things that they know about the other player.

It could be that after a few lines of Player 1 saying they know Player 2 has a crush on the gym teacher, Player 2 could retaliate by saying *'Well, do you know how I know that you killed the school rabbit?'* This second assertion could be based on something that has been said in the conversation already, or it could be something brand new.

#5: The conversation should continue back and forth with potentially multiple assertions being made about each other.

How Does the Game End?

The game ends when the Emcee feels they have made enough assertions about one another and the scene has reached a nice end point.

Alternatively, the players themselves could find the ending with the players acknowledging the other may be right/wrong or that they'll agree to disagree. They could then part ways and leave to show that the scene is over.

Pro Tips:

Pro Tip #1: Try playing the majority of the scene calmly. The characters could get upset or angry or excited at times, but the idea of the game is intended to be something of a polite or well-mannered conversation that carries an undertone of contempt for one another.

Pro Tip #2: You can make puns in the game to justify why the other character is what you are asserting them to be, but this isn't intended just as a joke telling game. So, you could have lines like *'you know how I know you like to save beavers? Because you're always nawty'*...but to be honest, I think this game is more suited to fun explanations rather than it just being about hitting puns.

6: STAY IN THE MOMENT

Emcee Intro Script: This game is called Stay in the Moment. In the game the players will perform a scene as if they are actors performing in a play. But they will have the challenge of keeping it going under some unusual circumstances that didn't happen in *"rehearsal"*. This can include the likes of lava slowly flowing onto the stage, or bats flying in through the window. They'll start the scene normally, and after a minute, I'll ask you for suggestions of what it is they're dealing with.

Challenge Style: Scene based

Players: 2+

Ask the Audience For: Before the scene starts, ask the audience for a suggestion of what the scene is about. This could be a theme or a location.

About a minute into the scene the Emcee should call *'freeze'* and the performers should pause the scene and physically freeze. The Emcee should then ask the audience for something that is about to start happening that will affect the performers' ability to continue the scene as they intended.

If you need to, give examples such as lava, one performer being possessed by a demon, one character having terrible foot cramp etc etc

How to Play the Game:

#1: The players start a normal scene based on the suggestion.

#2: After a minute, the Emcee calls *'freeze'* and takes a suggestion of something that will affect the performers being able to carry on with the scene.

#3: The performers continue the scene in the spirit of the show going on, but they should also demonstrate how they are clearly affected by what is now happening *(lava/bats etc)*.

Whatever the thing is, they should avoid directly referencing it as if they are attempting to keep the scene going as normal.

For example, if the scene was about a golf tournament, but the modifier is there is lava, they could show that they are hot, and their eyes are watering, but not directly mention the lava. They are trying to stay in the moment and should continue to make the scene about the golf tournament.

As the scene continues, they could start to react to their golf clubs being burning hot to touch and that the ball is on fire, but still try to continue the scene.

Eventually they could then be backed into a corner and end the scene panicking and standing on chairs, but still doing all they can not to break character.

How Does the Game End?

The Emcee should end the scene, ideally, whenever whatever is happening to affect the scene becomes overwhelming.

Pro Tips:

Pro Tip #1: The trick to this game is balancing the sense that you are continuing the scene that you started, but also doing enough to reference the new element (lava/bats/foot cramp etc)

Pro Tip #2: The characters could occasionally break character to acknowledge that something has happened, but quickly show they are doing their best to continue the scene.

Pro Tip #3: Contrast can be used to great effect in this game. A character mentioning that it is beautiful weather when the modifier is that there is a tornado or how cold you are whilst being melted by lava. Stuff like this will be fun.

7: HOTLINE

Emcee Intro Script: It's time to call the Hotline! What kind of hotline this may be is up to you! It could be some kind of business, or tech support. Maybe it's an entertainment hotline with the latest soap gossip or video game tips like you'd get in the 90s. Who knows? It could be a dating hotline or something a bit more...hot. The choice as always, is yours!

Challenge Style: Conversation

Players: 2

Ask the Audience For: What is the hotline for?

How to Play the Game:

#1: Two performers occupy half the stage each. Throughout the scene they should face towards the audience and not acknowledge that they can see each other. They can either hold physical phones or just mime them, but the idea is that their entire conversation will take place over the phone.

#2: One player takes on the role of the Hotline Worker, and the other takes on the role of a Customer who has called the hotline.

#3: To begin with, the Customer character should be happy to be on the call to speak to the Hotline Worker. This is because they were the one to initiate the call. This may change or evolve as the call progresses depending on the character of the Hotline Worker.

#4: The Hotline Worker should give unusual or unconventional advice for how to solve the Customer's problem or reason for calling.

How Does the Game End?

With one character hanging up the phone on the other.

Pro Tips:

Pro Tip #1: Decide who, if either player, is the quirky one. I would suggest as a rule of thumb, the Customer is portrayed as a normal person, and that the Hotline Worker is the unusual example of what they do. This of course could be flipped on its head and done the other way around.

It's possible that both players could be weird. This may not work as well as it may end up like a sandwich of bread filled with more bread. Doesn't work.

Pro Tip #2: Building off the last point, you could have the weirdness of the characters switch. This can be achieved by having the Customer seem normal at the start and part way through the call, the Hotline Worker becomes freaked out or concerned when the Customer is weirder than they are. If this happens, I'd endeavour to have the Hotline Worker tone down the quirkiness and realise the Customer is weird even to them.

8: COLD CALL

Emcee Intro Script: Oh no! It's now time for a game based on one of the most annoying things known to mankind...the Cold Call.

In this game one player will take on the role of an unsuspecting member of the public just minding their business and trying to get on with their day. The other will play the role of a Cold Caller, the spawn of Satan who will call you five minutes before the end of a movie to discuss solar panels. Or not care that it's 7am and want to ask about the road traffic accident that you had that wasn't your fault...even though you've never owned a car!

Challenge Style: Conversation/Objective based

Players: 2

Ask the Audience For: What is the Cold Caller calling about?

Note: This game works much the same way as the game Hotline, but almost in reverse. Instead of the Customer character needing advice or wanting to call the hotline, it is the Cold Caller who initiates the call. This means that the Customer may not be at all interested to hear what the Cold Caller has to say.

How to Play the Game:

#1: Player 1 is the customer and Player 2 is the Cold Caller. They should occupy one half of the stage each and act as if they cannot see each other. When the scene begins, the Customer should demonstrate that they are doing something which gets interrupted by the cold call. This could be sleeping, making dinner or collecting the kids from school.

#2: The Cold Caller should give a few seconds of the Customer doing whatever it is that they are doing before calling the Customer. The Cold Caller can mime a phone and say *'ring ring'* to start the call, or a sound effect can be used.

#3: The Cold Caller has a specific objective. That is to do all they can to keep the would-be Customer on the call for as long as they can.

The customer probably isn't interested in what the Cold Caller is selling or promoting, and it's up to the Cold Caller to use any tactic to keep the conversation going and make a sale.

How Does the Game End?

When either the Customer hangs up, or they agree to whatever the Cold Caller is calling about.

Pro Tips:

Pro Tip #1: The Cold Caller could call for genuine and good reasons, or they could be trying to pull off a scam, or anything in between. It doesn't always have to be that the call is nefarious. The audience could suggest that the call is a wrong number, or just that the person calling is lonely and wants a friend.

A cold-blooded cold call

9: PILLARS

Emcee Intro Script: It's now time to play Pillars. In this game, we'll need a couple of audience members to volunteer to help us, to be the pillars that our performers can lean on for support throughout the scene. Don't worry, they won't be physically leaning on you though. In the scene, the performers will occasionally point at our volunteers. If they do this, please give them a random word that they'll use to continue the scene.

Challenge Style: Scene based

Players: 2-4

Ask the Audience For: What the scene is about.

Setup: You could either get volunteers from the audience, or you could use two additional performers to give the random words. Either way, the people who will be saying the random words should stand either side of the performance area.

Each player in the scene should be assigned a specific volunteer who will provide random words for them when they are pointed at.

How to Play the Game:

#1: The players performing the scene should establish the scenario, location and characters for a good ten to twenty seconds.

#2: Once the scene is off and running, at any point, either performer in the scene can point to one of the volunteers stood at the side of the stage to get a random word. This word will be the next word that the performer will say in the scene.

#3: Performers can point to ask for a random word at any point, but it works best when the player has already started a sentence. The half sentence will often inspire the volunteer to come up with a random word. This can help, because if you point to them to get the first word of your sentence, they are less likely to conjure up an idea completely out of thin air.

How Does the Game End?

The Emcee should gauge when the scene has run long enough and end things before the audience grow tired of the concept.

Pro Tips:

Pro Tip #1: With the greatest of respect to the audience members, you can't always expect them to come up with something on the spot. Remember that they are not improvisers. So, there may be times where they don't think of something that is useful. It's therefore your job to try to use the words creatively to get the most out of them.

If they fail to say a word at all, you can brush this off as your character having blanked.

10: PILLARS – LIP READING EDITION

Emcee Intro Script: Our next game is a twist on the classic game of Pillars. In the traditional version of this game, performers have to periodically point to a volunteer from the audience. This volunteer would then tell the performer a random word they have to say in the scene.

This version of the game is very similar, but this time, we'll ask the audience member to just mouth the word and not actually say it out loud. Yes, our performers will have to lip read the volunteers and do their best to get the next word without actually being able to hear it.

Volunteers, after the performer has taken the word from you, I'd like you to give them the thumbs up if they understood your word correctly, or a thumbs down if they got it wrong. Either way, the scene will keep going.

Challenge Style: Scene based

Players: 2-4

Ask the Audience For: A location where the scene is taking place.

How to Play the Game:

#1: The audience members who are being lip read should be asked to position themselves slightly upstage of the performers and face towards the audience. This way, both the performers and the audience will be able to lip read them at the same time.

#2: The performers acting in the scene should perform it downstage of where the audience members are stood. Whenever a performer wishes to take a suggested word from the audience member, the performer should turn upstage to face the audience member so they can see their face.

The performer should then turn back towards the audience to deliver their next line, so they are not upstaging themselves.

#3: The humour in this scene comes from how accurate or inaccurate the performers are able to lip read the audience members, as well as how the random words may continue the story being told.

How Does the Game End?

When the Emcee feels it's run out of milage.

Pro Tips:

Pro Tip #1: I'd recommend the performers do their best to actually lip read and repeat what the audience member says accurately. If it is felt by the audience that the performer is purposely misreading the volunteer's words, they may feel cheated.

Of course, if the audience member says something rude, or undesirable for the performer to repeat, the performer could purposely misread their lips. In this instance, I would suggest you make it obvious that you are intentionally not going with what the audience member said.

Pro Tip #2: Remember to ask the audience members to show a thumbs up/thumbs down to indicate if the performers correctly read their lips or not. Whilst the performer's main priority should be to keep the story in the scene going, you can certainly find a game in which performer is better at reading lips.

11: ACTOR'S NIGHTMARE

Emcee Intro Script: We're going to play a game which is known as Actor's Nightmare. It will be a scene where one player is reading set lines form a script, and their scene partner is unscripted. Somehow, they have to do what they can to make the scene make sense.

Challenge Style: Scene based

Players: 2

Setup: You'll need a script that is suitable for this game already prepared. You'll have to find a scene where there are only two characters and decide which character the Scripted Performer will be reading. Ideally, there should be enough lines of dialogue for this game to be able to last a few minutes, and the scripted lines shouldn't include any monologues.

Ask the Audience For: It's not needed to ask the audience for any suggestions for this game. It is worth telling the audience what play or script you will be using for the scene though.

How to Play the Game:

#1: The Scripted Performer should read just their character's lines in order from their script.

#2: In between each scripted line, the Unscripted Performer should improvise their responses.

#3: Between the two players, there is the challenge to still make the scene sound natural and like it makes sense. The onus for this will primarily be on the Unscripted Performer as they are the ones who can deviate away from the set path of the scripted story.

This doesn't mean their aim is to simply guess at what the missing scripted lines would be, but they will have to shape all of their responses around the rigid scripted lines.

How Does the Game End?

It should end at the end of the scripted scene. The end point of the script that you are aiming towards can be worked out in advance of the show.

Pro Tips:

Pro Tip #1: The Scripted Performer may feel that they can't do much to gel with whatever the improvising Unscripted Performer says and does, but there are ways to help things gel together. The way the Scripted Performer reacts, their tone of voice and their physical behaviour are all up to the player. It's just the words they're not allowed to change.

Pro Tip #2: The Unscripted Performer needs to really listen and work within the confines of what the script allows them to do. There's no point saying you're jumping into your hot air balloon if the Scripted Performer makes it clear they are working in a café.

12: LOWER THE STAKES

Emcee Intro Script: We're going to Lower the Stakes! The performers will start in a scene of absolute catastrophe. With each passing line, they will have to find a way of lowering the stakes continually until everything in the scene is resolved and all is calm with the world again.

Challenge Style: Scene based

Players: 2

Ask the Audience For: Some kind of disaster or catastrophic event that will start the scene.

How to Play the Game:

#1: At the start of this scene, the players should make things as heightened and as dramatic as they possibly can.

#2: Then with every passing line, the characters should find ways to begin to tone things down. Respond to the events happening as if they're not world ending, and make discoveries that show things aren't as dramatic as they seemed.

#3: As you approach the ending of the game, you should start to find a place where the stakes are getting lower and lower. Keep this going until there really isn't anything of concern and any concerns and fears have been resolved.

How Does the Game End?

When the players have lowered the stakes so much that it feels like they can lower it no more, the Emcee should call it to finish.

Pro Tips:

Pro Tip #1: Keep in mind that this isn't a scene about time travel, or time running backwards. The things that seemed catastrophic at the beginning of the scene aren't erased or undone, and so therefore can continuously be referenced. It may just be that solutions were found, or that you were mistaken about the gravity of the situation.

13: CATHARSIS

Emcee Intro Script: I have a lot of built-up rage. Some frustration too. But it's OK, as this next game is about letting it all out. This game is called Catharsis, and will be a safe space for our performers to release any suppressed emotions.

Challenge Style: Scene based

Players: 2+

Ask the Audience For: An ordinary everyday activity.

How to Play the Game:

#1: The players will perform a scene, but as they are doing it, they should use whatever is happening in the scene to release and let go of any strong emotions the characters are carrying.

Respond to everything with sarcasm, a lack of gratitude, and with zero patience. For example:

Player 1: *Oh great...the sun is shining outside again. That's just what we need...*

Player 2: *Thanks for sharing...not! The wife will probably want to go out for a picnic now. And you know how much I love sitting in bugs and getting burned by the sun.*

Player 1: *Well maybe I should come with you, so I can hear all about the woes of you. That will cheer everyone up...*

#2: Just to be clear, this is still an improv acting scene and isn't intended as an actual exercise for the performers to deal with any real world issues they may have. I wouldn't recommend dealing with actual issues you haven't resolved during an improv show in front of an unsuspecting audience. Make sure whatever you do is clearly based on what the character is feeling and not yourself. If the audience think it's you being you, they may become uncomfortable.

#3: Even if a character is showing a lot of anger or frustration, or other strong emotions, I would say the other characters should take the release of the emotion in their stride. I would avoid making the whole scene about the characters getting cross at one another because the other person is showing frustration.

#4: You have the option of the characters being aware that they are letting all their emotions out, and that they are doing so in a therapeutic way. I would lean more towards the characters still trying to continue the story of the scene and carry on almost unaware that they are releasing such strong emotions.

How Does the Game End?

The Emcee can judge this.

Pro Tips:

Pro Tip #1: You could play the whole scene with negative emotions, but may be good to flow through different emotions slowly. Frustration may turn to full on anger, which when released is a feeling of relief then sadness then happiness for example. I'd avoid too much flip flopping back and forth between emotions as the idea is that you are going through them to release them and let them go.

Pro Tip #2: You need strong stage awareness and audience awareness with this game. Continually read the room for how what you are saying and doing is perceived by the audience.

14: TRY AGAIN

Emcee Intro Script: We're now going to have a scene for two performers. If either of the performers don't like the way the scene is going or what their fellow performer has come up with, they can interject and tell the other performer to *'Try Again'*. At this point, the other performer will have to *'try again'*.

Challenge Style: Scene based

Players: 2

Ask the Audience For: Something that the characters are doing.

How to Play the Game:

#1: The idea of this game is that during the scene any player can call out the phrase *'try again'* and their scene partner will have to come up with an alternative action or idea, or simply try the same idea again but to do it better.

If you're familiar with the game New Choice or the Extreme Improv variant Extreme Choices as featured in the original Extreme Improv Big Book of Improv Games, this game is similar, but not exactly the same in three major ways.

#2: One difference between New Choice and Try Again is that unlike in New Choice where an Emcee will be the person to call for new choices to be made, in Try Again, it is the players in the scene themselves who are calling upon their scene partners to come up with alternative choices.

#3: Another difference is that unlike in New Choice, the idea of trying again could be to come up with a new idea, or it could be to try the same idea again, but to do it with better results.

#4: Also, unlike New/Extreme Choices, calling *'try again'* doesn't erase the previously said line or action from the story. Because each player wants the other to try again when the phrase is called out, it adds the aspect of each player not being satisfied with what came before. This means that throughout the scene you can play with the idea of resenting each other or really wanting to please the other person.

#5: I would suggest letting the scene begin without either playing calling *'try again'* just so you can establish the scenario and who the characters are. Once you're twenty or thirty seconds in, I'd start to call try again after a player has said a line or taken an action. As the scene goes on, you can increase the frequency of how often you call *'try again'*.

How Does the Game End?

The game ends at the Emcee's discretion.

Pro Tips:

Pro Tip #1: Have fun with the duality of being both the performer and the character. The character may be ok with being asked to try again, but the performer playing the character may not. Experiment with how you can show this.

Find the game in trying to make the other actor try again...over and over. As the previous tries aren't erased from the script (*so to speak*), you can have fun with acknowledging that you keep making each other do new ideas again and again.

Pro Tip #2: Without doing it too much, I think there is also room to add suggestions of how you would like the other player to try again. You could say *'try again but angrier'* or *'try again sexier'*.

15: POSITIVE AND NEGATIVE

Emcee Intro Script: This game is called Positive and Negative and will be two scenes side by side that mirror each other. In the scenes one character will always be positive, and the other will always be negative.

Challenge Style: Scene based

Players: 2

Ask the Audience For: A profession or something the characters are doing that day.

The Emcee should also assign which player will do things positively and which will do thing negatively.

How to Play the Game:

#1: Player 1 will occupy one side of the stage, whilst Player 2 will occupy the other. The idea is that the performers are playing two similar, but different characters who will experience very similar events during their day. The difference will come in how they react and respond to things.

#2: The aim is that the two scenes will happen simultaneously. The players will have to pay close attention to what each other does and then incorporate similar events on their side of the stage.

#3: The scenes can involve dialogue but should only be one sided dialogue where the performers speak to invisible/mimed characters. For example, the characters could each speak to their boyfriends and say similar things to the mimed character. The way the performer speaks or reacts to the invisible character would then show how being positive or negative affects things differently.

#4: The performers should take care not to overlap their dialogue so that the audience can continuously keep track of both stories unfolding.

#5: The main objective for the performers is to show how each reacts to things that happen that make them feel either better or worse.

Here a few examples:

Both players may start the scene by waking up and realising that their alarms didn't go off. The positive player can brush this off as being pleased they got more sleep. The negative player may fear that waking up late will get them fired.

Both players may have a meeting with their boss at work. The negative one may make excuses for sloppy work and blame others, whilst the positive one may say that this has been a learning experience.

Both players may go on a hot date. The negative one may be annoyed to pay for an expensive meal, whilst the positive one relishes the opportunity to enjoy some fine dining.

How Does the Game End?

The game ends with the end of their day.

Pro Tips:

Pro Tip #1: Whilst the two characters shouldn't interact with each other, as the game is about seeing two contrasting days, there is the possibility that the two characters could cross paths momentarily. I would suggest that if the story lends itself to it, and there is a place where both characters may be traveling to, they could cross over to the opposite sides of the stage from where they each started and have a very brief interaction in the middle.

After this, the two players should continue their separate days on the other side of the stage. I wouldn't recommend doing this continually, and it would be something to practice in rehearsals.

Pro Tip #2: The game will be more about physicality and watching each character's body language and reactions rather than a focus on heavy dialogue. Try to keep things physical and have lots of action in it.

16: MUTATION

Emcee Intro Script: It's now time for Mutation. In this scene, there will be *'something'* that starts one way, but the longer the scene goes on, this *'something'* will become *'something else'* entirely.

For example, we may have a character who starts off as a girl scout, but by the end of the scene has to mutate into an opera singer. Or we may attempt to tell the story of Die Hard, but by the end it has to transform and mutate into A Christmas Carol. Maybe it's as simple as the hero becoming the villain. The choice is yours.

Challenge Style: Scene based

Players: 2+

Ask the Audience For: A suggestion of something that will mutate into something else by the end of the scene.

Feel free to ask for these elements individually as this will allow you to combine ideas that sound easier to work with.

How to Play the Game:

#1: The scene should start out quite normally. This is so you can establish to the audience what the starting point of the scene is before any mutation begins.

#2: As the scene progresses, the players should start to incorporate elements of whatever the scene or character is mutating into.

#3: By the end of the scene, the original suggestion should be completely removed and have fully transitioned over to whatever the second suggestion was.

How Does the Game End?

When the mutation is complete. Whatever the first suggestion was should be completely removed, and fully replaced by whatever the second suggestion was.

Pro Tips:

Pro Tip #1: The thing that mutates could be a story element that affects everyone, or it could be just one character that is mutating. Whatever the case may be, make sure that it happens gradually and not all at once.

Hammer: Hey! We nailed that scene!

Wrench: Really? I thought I'd thrown a spanner in the works!

17: ANYTHING YOU CAN DO I CAN DO BETTER

Emcee Intro Script: *(Singing)* Anything You Can Do, I Can Do Better…is the name of the next game. And it's about characters who will continuously try to one up and outdo each other.

Challenge Style: Scene based

Players: 2+

Ask the Audience For: A way that two people may know each other

How to Play the Game:

#1: The performers will start the scene fairly normally, but as the scene goes on, there will be an increased focus on doing things "better" or more elaborately than the other player. This may include repeating tasks that have already been done, or segueing off of what needs doing just to outdo the other character.

#2: Each character should react jealously or with desperation to prove they can outdo the other.

How Does the Game End?

When the scene reaches a heightened stage of ridiculousness where the characters are getting out of hand with their attempts to outdo one another.

Pro Tips:

Pro Tip #1: Don't allow yourself to get stuck just attempting to outdo one thing to the point that the scene cannot move forward. Find opportunities to concede that the other character did better, or act as if what they did doesn't matter, so that you can move the scene forward.

Allow time for something new to develop in the scene, and when a new opportunity comes up to try to outdo the other player…take it!

Pro Tip #2: Have fun finding the things you can't do better than the other player. This game lends itself to players showing off their hidden talents.

If a player were to do a standing backflip, or bust out some beat boxing, and you can't do these things, either just admit you can't do it, or try and fail. As always in improv, if you're going to fail, fail big! It'll be funny if you attempt to beat box or sing soprano in Italian and it sounds like a cat being slowly grinded through a mincer. Even if this is the case, you can still act confident like you think you were awesome.

And as for the backflip...yeah, maybe don't try that if you're not up to it. Safety first!

18: TOP THAT/THROW DOWN THE GAUNTLET

Emcee Intro Script: Our next game is Top That, also known as Throw Down the Gauntlet, and in the scene, there will be two very competitive characters who are always challenging one another to attempt to outdo things they are doing. Whenever an opportunity arises for a challenge, a character will throw down the imaginary gauntlet and challenge the other character to *'Top That'*.

Challenge Style: Scene based

Players: 2+

Ask the Audience For: A location or place of work.

How to Play the Game:

#1: Players start a scene based on the audience suggestion. I would suggest giving the scene at least twenty to thirty seconds to establish the characters before any challenges are made. Just set the scene and look for opportunities for the challenges to be created in the scene that follows.

#2: When you're ready, a character can do something and then throw down an imaginary gauntlet and challenge the other character to *'top that'*. This challenge can feel like it comes out of the blue, and the person being challenged may or may not be keen to accept the challenge. I would put emphasis on the challenge being a big deal.

Either way, once a challenge has been laid down, the player being challenged should attempt it even if they know they are going to fail.

#3: The challenges being laid out to one another can be anything really. Who can jump the highest, who can cross the road with most style. *"My yawn was the most audibly pleasing and you can never yawn quite so sweetly"*...stuff like this.

#4: If a player is successful at the challenge, the person who threw down the gauntlet could either be surprised, angry or humble and congratulatory to the other player.

#5: The scene should then continue until either player finds a new opportunity to lay down more challenges.

#6: The longer the scene goes on, the faster the challenges to top that should come. You can also increase the sense of competitiveness and that they are doing this for honour.

How Does the Game End?

The Emcee should judge when enough is enough and the scene has reached a good end point.

Pro Tips:

Pro Tip #1: You could act as if challenges being laid down are fun or trivial, but I think giving each challenge a sense of great importance is the way to go. If a challenged player sees that they are about to be challenged with the imaginary gauntlet being thrown down, they could beg them not to or react with a hushed silence.

Of course, a mix of reactions may be best overall, because if you act like every challenge has great gravity attached to it, it'll start to wear thin.

Pro Tip #2: If you have a glove or a gauntlet to use as a prop in the game this will help make the game feel more unique. Characters repeatedly reaching for and picking up the gauntlet to throw down again may be fun to play with.

Pro Tip #3: If the opportunity presents itself, it may be fun for both players to challenge each other at the same time. This could either be to do the same thing, or even do different things.

For example, one player could challenge the other to hold their breath as long as they can. Then before attempting this, the other player could challenge back, that they can hold their breath a lot longer than the other could keep running on the spot. This double challenge will create a fun sense of chaos.

19: WHO HAD IT WORSE?

Emcee Intro Script: Who Had It Worse? That is the name and theme for our next improv challenge. In this game, the players will attempt to achieve something, or carry out a task, whilst always finding ways to emphasise that their plight is worse than the other players. That's right, they're trying to win at failing to show they have suffered the most hardship.

Challenge Style: Scene based

Players: 2+

Ask the Audience For: Some kind of job, task or challenge the players are working to achieve.

How to Play the Game:

#1: The players start the scene and establish whatever the scene is about, what they are trying to achieve and who the characters are.

#2: The players need to find ways to highlight how they have things worse than the other player/s throughout the scene. This can be approached in numerous ways.

This can be done directly relating to things they are actively doing in the scene. For example:

Player 1: *(miming attempting to lift something heavy) I can barely lift this boulder.*

Player 2: *(also trying but doing it worse) Oof. That's easy for you to say. I cannot lift it at all.*

Alternatively, the characters could highlight why things are worse for them based on dialogue and stories from their past.

Player 1: *Attempting to lift this boulder reminds me of the time I broke my arm carrying a sack of bricks.*

Player 2: *You're lucky you were able to carry a sack of bricks. When I was young, my brother threw a sack of bricks at me, and I didn't manage to catch them and the bricks broke every bone in my body.*

Player 1: *You're lucky you were born with bones in your body. I was born with jelly fish disease and had to have surgery to put steel rods and chicken bones in all my limbs.*

#3: Make sure you find opportunities to move the scene forwards and not just get stuck in the first back and forth game of one upmanship...or is that one downmanship?

How Does the Game End?

The game ends when the stories and examples of how the characters have got things worse than one another became increasingly elaborate, and the Emcee feels they've topped out.

Pro Tips:

Pro Tip #1: Keep the characters doing things throughout the scene. If the scene just becomes a conversation about their life circumstances with nothing actively going on in the scene, you'll limit yourselves.

Pro Tip #2: So you don't just get stuck in a back and forth exchange, I would suggest that you keep the sense of outdoing one another quite casual. The aim isn't to be hyper competitive in this game. You could even deliver your stories of how you've had it worse with a sense of trying to gain sympathy from the other player. Another approach could be to show some degree of stoicism.

20: SAID NO ONE EVER

Emcee Intro Script: This game is my favourite improv game there is….Said No One Ever…We're now going to play a scene where at the end of every or most sentences, the players will have to end with the phrase *'said no one ever'*. You'll see how it works when we get into it!

Challenge Style: Scene based

Players: 2+

Ask the Audience For: A crime you would like to commit.

How to Play the Game:

#1: The players perform a scene, but most, if not every line has to end with the phrase *'said no one ever'*. This can either be said as a joke between the two characters or something they are in agreement about. Or it can be said under their breath as a way to disagree with the other character.

For example:

Player 1: *You make the best meatballs I've ever tasted…said no one ever.*

Player 2: *You're too kind. You've been the best dinner guest…said no one ever.*

Player 1: *Thank you. I'll be thinking about this night with you for weeks…said no one ever.*

How Does the Game End?

At the discretion of the Emcee.

Pro Tips:

Pro Tip #1: Not every line has to end with the phrase *'said no one ever'*. If you try to force it onto every line, you'll quickly find that the phrase doesn't work well with absolutely every type of sentence.

For example, saying *'said no one ever'* doesn't really work if tagged onto lines that are questions. It also doesn't need to be said after very short lines that are only there to help move the story of the scene on.

For example:

Player 1: *Scotland are going to win the World Cup....said no one ever.*

Player 2: *Can't argue with that...*

In the above example, the lack of the tag on phrase would probably get a laugh as the audience would soon start to expect that the phrase would be included on all lines. When it suddenly isn't there, it's exclusion would change the meaning of the line from sarcastic to genuine.

Pro Tip #2: As well as saying things that will sound mean or rude about the other player, you could use the phrase about your own character to be self-pitying. For example, *'everyone loves my ideas...said no one ever.'*

21: IF YOU KNOW WHAT I MEAN

Emcee Intro Script: We're now going to play a scene where at the end of every or most sentences, the players will have to end with the phrase *'if you know what I mean'*. This will imply some level of innuendo or some unsaid meaning.

Challenge Style: Scene based

Players: 2+

Ask the Audience For: A place where two people may meet.

How to Play the Game:

#1: Two players (or more) act out a scene where they will try to imply secondary meanings to most lines that they say. This can be achieved by a combination of a cheeky tone to their voice, and ending these lines of dialogue with the phrase *'if you know what I mean?'*

#2: Alternative phrases can be used at the end of lines, such as *'if you catch my drift'*, or *'I know you follow me here'*. Stuff like that. You can even mix up the formula with phrases at the start of lines of dialogue like *'I can see it in your eyes that...'*

#3: The phrase *'if you know what I mean?'* isn't really being said as a true question. Instead, it is being said with the assumption that the other character understands the secondary meaning of what is being said. For example:

Player 1: *It's getting 'hot' in here...if you know what I mean?*

Player 2: *Oh yeah...I can see my buns are rising, if you know what I mean?*

Player 1: *It's getting 'hard' not to see that, if you catch my drift?*

Player 2: *I can see it in your eyes that it's so warm you're getting a little sticky.*

How Does the Game End?

The Emcee can call *'and scene'* when they judge it has reached a good end point.

Pro Tips:

Pro Tip #1: Both the characters should generally understand each other's meaning, but it can be fun to occasionally take some of the innuendos literally.

Another option would be to purposely misunderstand the innuendo. This gives opportunity to have fun with misunderstandings.

Pro Tip #2: Make sure you include some physical action to support the dialogue of the scene. If everything you say has a secondary meaning, demonstrating a physical action can reveal if something being said is to be taken literally or not. For example, if a character actually is taking buns out of an oven, it will imply the secondary meaning is pure innuendo and they are actually baking buns.

22: TAG ON PHRASES

Emcee Intro Script: We're now going to combine two separate but similar improv games together. In this scene, the performers will be challenged to end their lines of dialogue with one of two phrases. Either *'if you know what I mean'* or *'said no one ever'*. You'll understand how they're using these phrases as we get into it.

Note: This game combines the rules of the previous two games featured in this book. If you were to play the previous two games within a show/workshop, this game would be a fun third game to play in a chain of games.

Challenge Style: Scene based

Players: 2+

Ask the Audience For: A place of work.

How to Play the Game:

#1: Players perform a scene where most sentences should end with a tag on phrase that will change the meaning of the dialogue said before it. These are:

Said No One Ever: This will imply you didn't mean the thing you have just said.

If you know what I mean?: This will reshape what you just said as an innuendo.

For fuller explanations of how these phrases can be used to good effect, please refer to the previous two games.

How Does the Game End?

At the judgement of the Emcee, once the scene has run for a few minutes.

Pro Tips:

Pro Tip #1: The fun thing with this game is that you can have an element of swerved expectations depending on the tag on phrase used.

For example, if we take the line :

Player 1: *It's getting hot in here…*

You could end it with either *'said no one ever'*, or *'if you know what I mean'* and it would really change the meaning depending on which you say.

You can use this tactic to play with both the expectations of the audience, and the expectation of the other player in the scene. Once you establish that their expectations may be swerved, you can then draw out your lines of dialogue as people will now be waiting to see which ending phrase you use.

23: SUSPICIOUS MINDS

Emcee Intro Script: We're now going to play a game called Suspicious Minds. In it, the characters are going to become suspicious after the other player has spoken a line of dialogue.

They'll challenge each other on what was meant by what they said and did, and question the other character's motives. They'll call each other out and suspect that the other character has other intentions beyond what the words alone suggest. Basically, they're going to continually misread each other.

Challenge Style: Scene based

Players: 2

Ask the Audience For: A type of relationship between two people.

How to Play the Game:

#1: The performers will start a scene to establish the characters and scenario.

#2: As the scene gets going, the characters should start to question the other character's motives for the things they say and do.

This can be pulled off through a questioning tone of their voice, and through suspicious looks and expressions. When challenging the motives of the other player, this can be done questioningly or accusingly.

For example:

Player 1: *It's a nice day to go for a jog, isn't it?*

Player 2: *A jog, eh? Are you trying to imply that I'm out of shape? That I need to work out more?*

Player 1: *Not at all. I just like jogging.*

Player 2: *Oh, OK then. I hope we run into Carla in the park.*

Player 1: *What are you getting at? There's nothing going on between me and Carla. How dare you?!*

How Does the Game End?

At the discretion of the Emcee.

Pro Tips:

Pro Tip #1: I think the characters in this game should move back and forth between being very suspicious and not really suspicious at all. Avoid the middle ground too much and be more one thing or the other.

It could be fun to overreact in a suspicious way at times. Player 1 could say something harmless that Player 2 reacts to, and the suspicion level could jump from zero to ten in an instant. Their reaction would be like a gotcha moment, or that they have caught out the other character.

Player 1 could then explain why what they said was intended as harmless, and just as instantly, Player 2 could drop their suspicion level to almost zero.

Certainly, you could go from two to eight, or thereabouts, but you shouldn't be constantly suspicious throughout the scene.

24: UNDER YOUR BREATH

Emcee Intro Script: It's really annoying when someone says something under their breath that you can't quite hear. I mean, why say it if you don't want me to hear? That's what this next game is all about.

Challenge Style: Scene based

Players: 2

Ask the Audience For: A place of work or a relationship between two people

How to Play the Game:

#1: The improvisers create a scene and as much or as little as they like, the characters should say things under their breath at the end of sentences that the other characters are not supposed to hear.

#2: Of course, as performers we do need to make sure the audience will hear. With this in mind, don't actually whisper or say things truly under your breath, but instead just say things in a lower voice or stage whisper. A stage whisper is that way of speaking so things have a hissy or whispery tone, but are still quite loud.

By doing a stage whisper, the audience will still understand what you are saying, but that the other player isn't meant to hear it.

#3: The characters should generally act like they don't hear the things each other say under their breath.

This said, you can also have fun with characters occasionally hearing something and questioning *'what did you say*?' The player who was overheard can then either lie about what they said, or make some excuse that nullifies it from being offensive to the character that heard it. The player that did overhear may continue to be sceptical that the other person is being rude or sneaky.

How Does the Game End?

When the Emcee feels the game has run its course.

Pro Tips:

Pro Tip #1: When you say things under your breath, you still need to be heard by the audience. You also need to make it clear when you are speaking under your breath.

One thing you can do to highlight when you are speaking under your breath is to slightly contort your mouth to show that you're slipping the words out of the corner of your mouth.

Another would be to turn your head slightly away from the person you're talking to. This way the audience can clearly see that you're not saying the words directly to them.

Pro Tip #2: You can have fun with the classic idea of saying *'the quiet part loud and the loud part quiet.'* By whispering the wrong thing, you can then say something out loud that you actually meant to whisper. Doing this will get you caught by the other character to humorous effect.

25: NO RHYME OR REASON

Emcee Intro Script: There is No Rhyme or Reason for this next game! But we're going to play it anyway! Two players will go back and forth with lines of dialogue. Each line they say must rhyme with a single word that the audience will suggest.

They're not allowed to use the same rhyming word more than once. Whoever makes a mistake first will lose the round. This game will have five rounds, with each round based on a different word.

Challenge Style: Scene based

Players: 2

Ask the Audience For: Random words

How to Play the Game:

#1: The two players perform a scene where each line of dialogue must rhyme with the word suggested by the audience.

#2: The players keep going until a player fails to rhyme with the word suggested by the audience. This can be by saying a word that doesn't rhyme, taking too long to think of a rhyme, or saying a word that does rhyme that has been used before.

#3: Homophones are allowed. As an example, this means you can rhyme the word *'two'* with *'too'* and *'to'*. Be warned though that the different word should be as clear as possible from the context of your line of dialogue.

For example:

Player 1: *I know where to send that to.*

Player 2: *That's ok cause I know too.*

Player 1: *Great so I'll send two.*

The context of the example sentences makes it clear which word is being used to end each line. Advanced players could purposely make it ambiguous without breaking the rules. For example, the following line:

Player 1: *You bought one, I want to buy two.*

Could also be heard as the following:

Player 1: *You bought one, I want to buy too.*

#4: If there is a dispute over the usage of a word the player should be given a brief moment to justify their usage of the word. If they cannot clarify this within five-ten seconds, or if the player repeatedly uses words that can be disputed the Emcee should rule against them. This may not seem fair, but it is in the interest of maintaining the flow of the game.

#5: As soon as a player goes wrong, the Emcee should award a point to the player who won the round. The Emcee should then quickly get another word from the audience and start another round.

#6: Players should take turns at who has to start each round.

#7: This game should last the full five rounds – even if it's 4-1 or 5-0 by the end. In these instances, even once it's become apparent that the losing player cannot come back and even the score, you should keep playing to see the whole game through.

How Does the Game End?

This game ends once the fifth and final round has been won by one of the players.

Pro Tips:

Pro Tip #1: This game should be played with a fairly rapid pace. If a line of dialogue feels too long for the rhyme to feel natural, this should be called as a fail.

Pro Tip #2: As every word will only have a finite number of rhyming words there is no need to artificially throw the fight as someone will inevitably lose. This said, you could purposely lose a round if there is an opportunity to get a big laugh by going wrong. Ultimately the aim is to make the game fun and entertaining.

SECTION 2: ONE PLAYER GAMES

Want some games to practice on your own? How about some fun monologue games to showcase a single player in a show? We've got you covered. All of the games in the following section are designed so they can be played with just one performer.

You never have to share the spotlight in a Soloprov show!

26: FORTUNE TELLER

Emcee Intro Script: I can see into the future! And I can see that our next game is Fortune Teller. One of our performers will take on the role of a fortune teller to read the mind and soul and tell the future to one lucky individual.

Challenge Style: Character based

Players: 1

Ask the Audience For: Ideally, you should ask for a volunteer to have their fortune told.

Alternatively, you could ask the audience for a suggestion of a celebrity, well known personality, or entity like a company or sports team.

Setup: All of these are optional, but you could have a table for the fortune teller to sit at, and could have props like a crystal ball, or tarot cards.

How to Play the Game:

#1: The player telling the fortune should ideally be sat at a table but could be without a table or just stood.

#2: You have the option to bring a volunteer on stage, or you could address a person in the audience. Either way, if you are telling the fortune of someone from the audience, you should ask them questions to get to know a few details about them.

This can include their name, what they do for a living, if they are at the show with anyone, what their relationship status is, and maybe what their hobbies are.

#3: Based on the information you get; you should give responses that show you already knew or suspected certain things about them. Highlight when you get things right, or question if they are being truthful if you get things wrong. The persona for the fortune teller should lean towards being mysterious and all knowing.

#4: Once you have gathered some information, you should go into predicting their future. This can be anything you make up, but you should try to weave in details that you have learned about them to make it sound more personal to the individual. Doing this will help keep the game feeling personal and interactive.

How Does the Game End?

The game can be ended by the player who is performing as the fortune teller. They should be the ones to bring it to a conclusion in a suitably mysterious way.

Pro Tips:

Pro Tip #1: You have the option to read the palms of the volunteer, or use tarot card props to enhance the idea that you are a mind reader. Other things you can do is go into a trance, conduct a séance, or get the person to engage in chanting with you. There's lots of things that people associate with these kinds of mystical readings.

Pro Tip #2: Be careful about getting too personal with audience members if you are commenting on things that could be sensitive. For example, you shouldn't hold a séance to speak to a family member of the audience who has passed away. I would also say to tread carefully if predicting bad things will happen to them in the future if they are someone who may turn out to be superstitious.

Pro Tip #3: You have more free reign to say outlandish or over the top things if telling the fortune of a company or celebrity.

Pro Tip #4: If you're talking about a celebrity, a company or sports team, and telling their fortune, I would suggest you still engage with the audience where possible. Ask questions about who does or doesn't like the team or celebrity, and say that you sense a lot of love/hate from certain people in the room.

27: JUST KEEPING RHYMING

Emcee Intro Script: Just. Keep. Rhyming! This is a game where our players will be given a word or phrase, and then they'll have to create a monologue of sorts where everything they say must keep rhyming with the suggested word or phrase. The game will end when they have clearly run out of steam or just start repeating themselves.

Challenge Style: Monologue/Poem

Players: 1

Ask the Audience For: A word or a phrase

How to Play the Game:

#1: Once the player has the suggestion from the audience, they should begin their monologue.

#2: The player has to ensure that the lines of their monologue continue to keep rhyming with the suggested word or phrase.

#3: Remember that the game is about performing a monologue and isn't just about performing a poem. You should talk in the first person, and make what you're saying about your character. Don't fall into the trap of just telling a story because you're rhyming.

How Does the Game End?

The game can be ended by the player themselves if they feel they have clearly reached the end of the story they're telling. Alternatively, the Emcee can interject to end it themselves. The Emcee should do this if the player is using the same words over and over again.

Pro Tips:

Pro Tip #1: You can bend the rules slightly by using half rhymes, or slightly mispronouncing words so that they rhyme with the audience suggestion. I suggest that this is something that you should do sparingly.

If you break this rule too often, the audience will lose track of what the actual rhyming word is, and it won't be obvious when the monologue should end.

Pro Tip #2: The game is about performing a monologue, so don't be afraid to use all of your acting skills. Show different emotions, use contrast, play around with physicality, pace and volume. Have fun with it.

Don't forget to run...the games in rehearsals...

28: BEAT POEM

Emcee Intro Script: Our next game is Beat Poem. One player is about to open your mind and bare their soul in a stylish and stylised poem.

Challenge Style: Poetry

Players: 1 *(with optional musical accompaniment)*

Ask the Audience For: A theme for the poem

Setup: Beat poems are often performed with an undercurrent beat, usually with a jazz vibe. This can either be underscoring the poem, or as musical breaks between verses. If you have someone who can play an instrument to add this effect that would be best, but you can also use backing tracks.

How to Play the Game:

#1: Once the player has the suggestion, they should take centre stage to perform the poem.

#2: The poems are usually a direct address to the audience. This style of poem lends itself to self-expression and raw emotion.

#3: Beat poems don't usually rhyme, but this is a rule which I feel is ok to break if you are comfortable hitting rhymes.

#4: Even if your beat poem doesn't rhyme, you should still aim for the language to flow and a sense of rhythm in your speech.

How Does the Game End?

The player performing the Beat Poem should be the one to draw it to a close. A minute or two is usually plenty.

Pro Tips:

Pro Tip #1: As this game is about replicating the style of a Beat Poem, I'd say the best thing to do is research a few online to get a sense of the style, rhythm, and the persona that goes with it.

Pro Tip #2: Even though this style of poem is based on free expression, you should still aim to have a structure to the poem you are performing.

The start should introduce the concepts, themes and characters you will be covering. Is your poem about a personal experience? An issue in society? The start should introduce what you're talking about and give insight into why you're talking about it.

The middle section should be the longest and should be about exploring these themes in more detail. Expand on things that have happened and your reaction to them. Identify problems, and who is to blame.

The ending should aim to be a conclusion of sorts. This can include saying how something was resolved or be a mission statement for what needs to be done next.

Pro Tip #3: Take your time. It's good to have some pace on the poem, but it can be easy to let the sense of passion and raw emotion make these seem like a rant, and race through dialogue.

You should play with the speed level. If you have some light jazz music in the background it can help set the pace.

Pro Tip #4: If you do wish to include music, it is better if it can be played live rather than just using a backing track, but use what you can. A live musician can respond to the performer's pace and tone to compliment it, where as a prerecorded track will be fixed. This can mean that you end up matching the track rather than the track match you.

29: INDECISIVE THOUGHTS

Emcee Intro Script: Our next game is called Indecisive Thoughts. In the game, one player will perform a monologue where they are thinking over an idea or topic, or debating something that they should or should not do. But…every time I *(the Emcee)* ring this bell *(or buzzer)* they will have to change their mind entirely and ramble on all the reasons why the idea was bad, or they shouldn't do it.

Challenge Style: Monologue

Players: 1

Ask the Audience For: Something the player wants to achieve.

How to Play the Game:

#1: The player begins their monologue about what it is they want to achieve and how they plan to do it.

#2: The Emcee should listen carefully to the monologue and pick places to either ring a bell/buzzer or call the word *'change.'* When this happens the player doing the monologue can suddenly flip the direction of the speech like they are having indecisive thoughts.

#3: The monologue can include a little information that is world building but should not focus on it. This will give a sense of who their character is, and where/when they are. This should be covered briefly, but the bulk of the monologue should be more focussed on something they are doing or planning to do.

#4: Avoid the monologue just being a story about something that happened in the past. You could make that work, but it would be better to see your character trying to achieve something or resolve a current conflict rather than just explain their past decision making. But with practice, you could make either approach work.

How Does the Game End?

The game ends when the monologue feels it's reached something of a resolution. Maybe one to two minutes in length would be appropriate for the story to have been explored enough. It could be that the player makes it clear when the end has been reached, or the Emcee can make a judgement call as to when it's hit a nice crescendo or ending point.

Pro Tips:

Pro Tip #1: Unlike the games New Choice or Extreme Choices *(featured in the Extreme Improv Big Book of Improv Games)*, your previous dialogue isn't 'erased from the script' in this game. The new thoughts don't mean you didn't say the previous ones. It's just that your character has changed their mind.

This means you can continue to reference your previous thoughts, or still consider ideas that you've rejected.

Pro Tip #2: The ending of the monologue could come with a big and dramatic moment, or it could come with something more sombre and thoughtful.

Pro Tip #3: When it looks like the ending, the Emcee could suddenly call *'change'* one last time and the player could start back up again. This is what is known as a false finish.

If you do a false finish, this could be for just a short joke, or you could keep it going for another twenty or thirty seconds until you reach another ending.

Also, if you do a false finish be careful not to milk things too much by going on for too long. Better to end the game whilst the audience are still enjoying it rather than outstay your welcome.

Variation: This could be a two-player game where one person is giving advice to another and rapidly changes their minds and gives alternative advice.

30: MELTDOWN

Emcee Intro Script: We are now going to play Meltdown. One player will take on the role of a well-respected professional, or member of society who is about to deliver a speech in front of a room full of people. One snag. Moments before going on stage they have received some bad news and will have to attempt to give the speech as unaffected by this news as possible.

Challenge Style: Monologue

Players: 1

Ask the Audience For:

#1: A suggestion of who the character is. This doesn't need to be a specific individual and could just be someone from a profession or field who is giving a speech at some kind of event. It could be an awards event, or a charity event or some kind of conference.

#2: A suggestion of what the bad news the character will receive is. This could be something serious like they've been fired, the police have figured out they're a criminal, their partner is cheating on them, a death etc. Or it can be something less serious like their favourite football team lost, the milk has gone bad or a TV show has been cancelled.

I would shy away from a death for the suggestion if you can. I think this will be where the audience's mind goes to first, and it runs the risk of the monologue just being about sadness or over the top crying.

How to Play the Game:

#1: The player should walk to centre stage ready to give their speech.

#2: You have two options here. Either the player walks to centre stage having already received the bad news, or another player/the Emcee could walk up to them and whisper the bad news to them just as they're starting.

#3: The player should attempt to compose themselves and deliver the speech they intended to before they received the bad news. The longer the speech goes on, the more they should not be able to hide their feelings on the news.

#4: I would suggest that the player avoids directly acknowledging or addressing the bad news to the audience and that it's never said until the very end, if at all. Keep in mind that the audience already know what the bad news you're dealing with is. The aim of the game is to watch the character meltdown. Even though the audience already know what the bad news is, the logic is that the audience your character is addressing wouldn't know it.

How Does the Game End?

The game can either be ended by the Emcee, or by the performer themselves.

The Emcee could interject and make an excuse for the speaker needing to leave as they are clearly not feeling well.

Alternatively, the performer could end it if they reach a natural end point to the speech. They would probably need to thank the audience for listening and excuse themselves to leave whilst aware that they went overboard.

Pro Tips:

Pro Tip #1: It could be fun to attempt to continue talking about whatever the speech is supposed to be about but at the same time make the subtext of the speech about whatever the bad news is.

For example, if the bad news was that someone was cheating on you, and you're meant to be talking about your long career raising money for dolphins, you could get something like this:

Player 1: *Today marks the tenth year I've worked for this charity. Ten years is a long time. But I believe in loyalty. Not everyone does, but I do. Loyalty. Dolphins are loyal too. And they appreciate everything you do for them. Dolphins don't go off with Steve from work when my back is turned!*

Pro Tip #2: The character could use the bad news as a point of revelation in their life, and give them new perspective and clarity. This could result in them being sad, bitter or even poignant.

The speech could easily turn into a rant, but this game also gives room for the player to go deep and meaningful with it. The aim of the game is for it to be fun and entertaining and not become a lecture, but certainly, there is room for something slightly more meaningful here if the scenario lends itself to it.

SECTION 3: LANGUAGE LIMITATIONS

These games are all ones that will challenge your command over language. Restrictions and limitations encourage creativity, and in all of these games you'll have to be creative with your use of language.

Embrace making an ass of yourself on stage!

31: BANNED LETTER

Emcee Intro Script: It's now time for the Banned Letter Game! There will be two performers in the scene at any time. As much as possible, they'll have to avoid saying any words that contain a letter of the alphabet that we will shortly ban.

If they say any words that contain a banned letter, they will be eliminated from the game! If they hesitate for too long, or have what we deem to be a circular conversation they will be eliminated from the game. Every forty-five seconds we will ban an additional letter.

Challenge Style: Scene based/Competitive

Players: 2+

Ask the Audience For:

A scenario for the characters. Can be a place of work or an activity.

Also ask for what letter should be banned when the game begins. Freeze the scene and ask for an additional letter every forty-five seconds.

How to Play the Game:

#1: If a player says any words that contain a banned letter, they are instantly eliminated from the game and replaced in the scene with another player.

#2: The players are not allowed to hesitate. This means leaving anything longer than a very short pause between lines of dialogue. It also means speaking at a very slow pace or regularly just giving one or two words as their line of dialogue.

#3: Players are not allowed to have a circular conversation. This means lines of dialogue that just use the same words over and over, and doesn't continue to move the scene forward. A player should also avoid repeating back the line just said by the other player and only adding one or two words. Doing this would count as circular. For example:

Player 1: *Is the dog in the house?*

Player 2: *Is the dog in the house you ask? Yes.*

If a player is thought to be creating a circular conversation, the Emcee can issue a warning in the first instance, or can eliminate a player.

#4: If a player is eliminated, a new player should enter the scene as a new character.

#5: Every forty-five seconds, the Emcee should call *'Freeze'* and ask the audience for another letter which will be banned. The new banned letter is stacked, so multiple letters end up banned at once.

How Does the Game End?

When all but one player have been eliminated leaving one as the winner.

Pro Tips:

Pro Tip #1: For the Emcee, I would suggest not allowing more than one vowel to be banned. To do so will quickly make the scene too difficult for the players.

Pro Tip #2: I would also advise that if the audience only suggest less commonly used letters like Z, Q, X, J or K that it will make the game too easy.

Pro Tip #3: For players in the scene, you can have fun trying to get the other player to make mistakes. You can do this by asking them questions where the answer will obviously include the banned letter.

Pro Tip #4: I would also suggest that players really avoid being too careful in this game. Winning is nice, but if you take it too seriously, the game could potentially go on forever. The aim of the game isn't to win, but to make the scene entertaining and fun for the audience. Don't be afraid to speak fast and risk making mistakes rather than speaking slow and too carefully.

32: RIDDLE ME THIS

Emcee Intro Script: Our next game is Riddle Me This. In the game, one performer will speak almost exclusively in riddles, whilst all the others try to have a normal conversation with this Riddler.

Challenge Style: Scene based

Players: 2-5

Ask the Audience For: A reason why people come together to meet.

The Emcee can either assign which performer should be the Riddler, or ask the audience to pick.

How to Play the Game:

#1: The players should start the scene and establish the scenario.

#2: Periodically, the other characters should speak to the Riddler who should only speak in riddles and indirect ways. For example:

Player 1: *Which team are you supporting tonight?*

Player 2: *I've always been a Manchester United fan myself. How about you?*

Riddler: *The team who gets my support, are the team who are a collection where weapons rest, a place where strength is amassed...*

Player 1: *Yes, I'm supporting Arsenal as well.*

#3: You have the choice whether the other characters simply understand what the Riddler is saying, or is confused by their choice of language. A mix of both is fine.

I would suggest that between the players, you should always make sure the audience understand what the answer to the riddles were. This can be achieved by players guessing or confidently stating the answer to the riddles. Either way, the Riddler should nod to confirm, or correct what the answer is if the other players don't know what is meant.

How Does the Game End?

The Emcee should look to end the scene at a high point.

Pro Tips:

Pro Tip #1: The Riddler should ideally be someone who is confident that they can talk in a mysterious and figurative manner. This is something that can be developed and worked on in rehearsals.

Here's a few more examples, so you can see how the riddles could work.

Apple: *I hear a buzzing from the forbidden fruit, and from which voices come from within.*

Car: *I am a horseless wagon, powered by liquid, but we call it gas. What am I?*

Mother: *She who burdened my weight and carried me for three quarter of a year.*

Computer keyboard: *I have keys but no locks, space but no room, and you can enter but not go outside.*

Clock: *I go around in circles, but always move forward, and my hands clap only at hour intervals.*

Pro Tip #2: The other players can choose how they react to the riddles. Maybe to them it's just normal to hear, or maybe they get frustrated with the Riddler's lack of clarity by not giving simple responses.

Pro Tip #3: The Riddler can have fun by being mysterious. You can choose if they're an unusual kind of being, or if they're doing this for attention.

Pro Tip #4: The Riddler doesn't have to speak 100% in riddles. When clarifying things, they could drop the mysterious persona which should generate a laugh here or there. It could also be that they suddenly go into speaking in riddles whenever they want to be dramatic or the centre of attention but could still give short answers in a normal way at other times.

33: TWO LINES

Emcee Intro Script: Our next improv challenge is called Two Lines, and is a scene for three performers. In the game, two of our performers will be limited to only be able to say two lines of dialogue each. They can say these two lines as many times as they'd like, but they aren't allowed to say anything else.

The third player will then be allowed to say anything they wish throughout the scene. Their goal is to keep the scene going and make it all make sense.

Challenge Style: Scene based

Players: 3

Ask the Audience For: Firstly, where the scene is set.

Secondly, ask the audience for the two lines of dialogue that each of the first two players can say. Each player gets two different lines, so you'll need four lines of dialogue in total. These should be short lines like *'I'm not feeling very well'* or *'I'd love to'*.

How to Play the Game:

#1: A lot of the responsibility for the scene to make sense will come from the player who can say anything they like. As such, they should do most of the work to establish the scenario and what the characters are doing.

#2: Along the way, the two performers who are limited to speaking the lines they have been assigned should find any opportunities to speak their lines within the context of the scene. The idea is that the lines should be said to make sense, and shouldn't just be said as gobbledygook.

How Does the Game End?

When the Emcee feels the scene has reached the end of its story, or that it has run long enough.

Pro Tips:

Pro Tip #1: If you are a player who has the limitation of just saying two lines, you'll need to be creative in how you say them. Find as many ways to say the same words, but tweak the meaning with the tone of your voice and intention.

Pro Tip #2: Players can also just be physical and use body language to show how they're feeling if the exact lines don't work with what is going on at the time. This said, the audience will be watching and waiting to see the different ways you find to say the lines, so don't avoid saying them completely to just be physical.

Feel free to go nuts and enjoy playing Two Lines!

34: RHYMING ALPHABET SCENE

Emcee Intro Script: It's now time for the Rhyming Alphabet Scene! Each time the players start a new line of dialogue, the line will have to start with the next letter of the alphabet. In addition to this, the lines of dialogue should rhyme.

Challenge Style: Scene based

Players: 2

Ask the Audience For: A problem that you have caused recently.

Also, a letter of the alphabet for the players to start at.

How to Play the Game:

#1: Players are assigned as Player 1 and Player 2.

#2: Player 1 starts the scene with an opening line of dialogue.

This line of dialogue will have to begin with a word that starts with the letter of the alphabet that was suggested by the audience. For this example, we'll say they suggested the letter 'A'.

#3: After Player 1 has said a line, it is Player 2's turn to speak. Their line will have to start with a word that begins with the next letter of the alphabet *(in this instance B),* and line will also have to rhyme with the last line said by Player 1.

#4: The game will continue in this pattern for the remainder of the scene.

How does the game end? The game ends when the players have gone all the way through the alphabet.

How Does the Game End?

The scene should play out until all letters of the alphabet have been used to start a line of dialogue. The players should attempt to wrap up the story within the last few lines.

Variations: You have the option to put a time limit on this game as is common with other variations of Alphabet Scenes. This is usually ninety seconds or two minutes. I'd be tempted not to put this limit on the performers as this game is focussed on the rhyming aspect and not just getting through the alphabet.

Pro Tip/Advanced Method

I have said that Player 2 must always rhyme with Player 1. This doesn't have to be the case. If you have players who are confident to do so, both players can rhyme with each other in a more free flowing manner.

To do this, players should extend their lines beyond the rhyme. This way they'll also set up a new rhyme for the other player.

Here's an example. The rhyming words will be highlighted in caps to make the pattern easy to follow.

Player 1: *Hello pal, do you wanna PLAY?*

Player 2: *I sure do, if I MAY? Do you want to play BALL?*

Player 1: *Joe, you bet! And that's not ALL! I also want to SWIM.*

Player 2: *Killer! But gosh I forgot my swimming shorts. I'm so DIM.*

Player 1: *Lol my dude. You can borrow MINE.*

Player 2: *Man, that's great! If you're sure that's FINE? I'll owe you ONE.*

Player 1: *No worries. Now let's have some FUN.*

As you'll see from the short example above, the players didn't use a set pattern for if they rhymed with the previous player. Sometimes they rhymed in the middle of a line, and then set up the next rhyme, and sometimes they didn't.

Doing this is an advanced technique, but will add some variety to the rhyming pattern.

35: ALLITERATION ALPHABET SCENE

Emcee Intro Script: Our next game is what is known as an Alliteration Alphabet Scene. Every time a player starts a new line of dialogue, every word in that line will have to start with a single letter of the alphabet only. For example, every word in the first line may have to begin with the letter A. Then in the second line said by the other player every word would have to begin with B. And so on with C, D etc...

Challenge Style: Scene based

Players: 2

Ask the Audience For: Something you were given as a present that you didn't like.

How to Play the Game:

#1: Player 1 will say a line of dialogue where all the words in the line begin with the letter A.

#2: After this, Player 2 must begin all the words in their line with the letter B.

#3: This pattern continues until they have gone all the way through the alphabet.

#4: The idea is to make the scene continue to make sense and not just be a list of words. Listening is key, and you'll have to find ways to reference things that have already been said earlier in the scene. This is keeping in mind that you won't be able to repeat anything that has already been said, as you'll be using a new letter for each line.

Example scene:

Player 1: *Ahhhh! Angry Angela attacked Aaron.*

Player 2: *Body blows? Broken bones? Blood?*

Player 1: *Complete catastrophe.*

Player 2: *Damn...Dead? Do disclose details David.*

Player 1: *Eviscerated.*

Modifiers:

Like other variations of Alphabet Scenes, you could ask the audience for a specific letter of the alphabet for the players to begin at. The scene could also be timed with a traditional ninety seconds for the players to attempt to get all the way through the alphabet.

How Does the Game End?

Once the players have gone all the way through the alphabet.

Pro Tips:

Pro Tip #1: Don't be afraid to use slight pauses as changes in thought. This can make otherwise disjointed sentences seem to make more sense. It will just come off as you thinking between words rather than skipping words that don't start with the current letter. Be warned though, if you do this constantly, it'll grow old fast.

Pro Tip #2: If you are able to do some longer sentences in this game, it will be impressive. Avoid all sentences being just one or two words long.

Pro Tip #3: You can very very occasionally cheat and say a word that starts with the wrong letter if doing so will get a laugh. If you do this though, I would be tempted to make it obvious to the audience that you know you went wrong or are cheating.

For example, saying *'Rachel really wrote'* sounds alliterative, but in terms of the rules of the game, not all of those words began with an R.

Pro Tip #4: Another fun way to cheat is by purposely pronouncing a word incorrectly.

For example, *'Becky borrowed Ben's banana but broke Ben's botatoes'*. You'll get a laugh with something like this, and once again, you should in some way acknowledge that you know you're attempting to pull a fast one.

36: ALPHABET SCENE DJ

Emcee Intro Script: We're now going to play Alphabet Scene DJ. Our performers are going to create a scene where every time they start a new line of dialogue it has to begin with the next letter of the alphabet. A followed by B followed by C.

But as this game is called Alphabet Scene DJ, it has a twist. I *(the Emcee)* will be the DJ of this scene, and can decide at any time to call out *'forward'* or *'reverse'* and the alphabet will now go in that direction. So sometimes the alphabet will go backwards and they may end up having to use the same letters many times over.

Challenge Style: Scene based.

Players: 2 plus the Emcee.

Ask the Audience For: Something that needs fixing.

How to Play the Game:

#1: Player 1 says a line of dialogue that starts with a word that begins with the letter A.

#2: Player 2 then says a line of dialogue that starts with a word that begins with the letter B.

#3: This pattern continues, but at any point, the Emcee can call out instructions like *'Forward'* or *'Reverse'* to change the direction of the alphabet.

For example, if a player had just said a line that began with the letter D, and the Emcee calls *'Reverse'*, the next line should now begin with the letter C. The players should continue going backwards through the alphabet until the Emcee calls out *'Forward'* again.

For clarity, in this game, the Emcee calling out these instructions only changes the direction of the alphabet. It does not mean that the players have to repeat dialogue that was already said as you would in the game known as Forward Reverse.

#4: The Emcee can also call out *'Skip to…'* and then say a random letter for the players to pick the game up from.

How Does the Game End?

Once the players have gone all the way through the alphabet.

Pro Tips:

Pro Tip #1: This game could potentially keep going on forever. As such, I would suggest that the Emcee does allow the players to eventually get all the way through the entire alphabet in one direction or another. This will add a sense of completeness.

Pro Tip #2: The Emcee could change up their persona and actions to mimic a DJ from a night club to add to the presentation of the game.

37: MEET IN THE MIDDLE ALPHABET SCENE

Emcee Intro Script: We're now going to play a Meet in the Middle Alphabet Scene! Two players will perform a scene where each time they say a new line of dialogue it will have to begin with the next letter of the alphabet...but here's a twist.

One of the performers will start at the letter A and go through the alphabet in the order ABC, but the other player will start at Z and have to go through the alphabet backwards, ZYX and so on. If they're both doing it correctly, they will meet in the middle!

Challenge Style: Scene based

Players: 2

Ask the Audience For: A type of event you could get tickets for.

How to Play the Game:

#1: Player 1 will start each line of dialogue with a word that begins with the subsequent letter of the alphabet starting at the letter A. Their first line will start with A, their second line will start with B, third with C and so on.

#2: Player 2 will start at the end of the alphabet, starting with Z. Their first line with start with the letter Z. Their next line will start with Y, followed by X, then W, etc etc.

#3: Eventually, the players will meet in the middle, on M and N. You have the option to end the game here, or the players could continue the scene all the way through until Player 1 has reached Z, and Player 2 has reached A.

How Does the Game End?

Once the players have made it to the specified end point. This will either be the middle of the alphabet, or the longer version where they reach the opposite end of the alphabet to which they started.

See Also: In the original Extreme Improv Big Book of Improv Games there are several variations of the Alphabet Scene game including traditional and Reverse variations. Both of these will provide valuable insights that can enhance your playing of this version, and vice versa.

Pro Tips:

Pro Tip #1: Playing any version of an Alphabet game can highlight to many an improviser how poorly we all remember the alphabet.

If you are the player going forwards with the alphabet, you have it easier. If you are going backwards, you have the more challenging task.

My biggest tip for both players is that as soon as you finish a line of dialogue, you should quickly cue yourself on what your next letter needs to be.

So, if you've just finished a line that started with the letter A, you should think '*AB*' in your head, to make sure you have the letter B ready to go. After your second line just think '*BC*'. Follow this pattern and you'll never get lost.

Likewise, if you're going in reverse, think *ZY* after your first line to make sure you have the letter Y loaded up and ready to go. Then *YX*, then *XW*, then *WV* etc.

Pro Tip #2: Make sure you always keep listening to the other player's dialogue. Players often make the mistake of just concentrating on what the next letter is and forget to listen to what else is going on in the scene.

Even if you take a moment to cue up the next letter, it's more important that you always listen to what your scene partner is adding to the scene and be present.

Pro Tip #3: Emcee, it can be worth telling the audience to shout the next correct letter at the performers if they get lost with the alphabet. This will make it more interactive, and also add to the fun rather than seem awkward if the performers get stuck.

38: EVIL ALPHABET SCENE

Emcee Intro Script: Our next game is what is known as the Evil Alphabet Scene. Two performers will create a scene, which could be about anything, but there are two rules.

Firstly, as seen in a traditional Alphabet Scene, the players have to start each line of dialogue with the next letter of the alphabet. A followed by B, followed by C, and so on. The other rule is that every line of dialogue must start with a word that can be considered evil or dastardly.

Challenge Style: Scene based

Players: 2

Ask the Audience For: A project the characters are working on.

You should also ask the audience what letter of the alphabet the performers should start at.

How to Play the Game:

#1: Two players start the scene.

#2: Whichever player says the first line of dialogue will have to start that line with a word that begins with the letter A *(or whatever letter the audience specified they should start from.)*

#3: The other player should then start their next line with a word that starts with the next letter of the alphabet. So, if the first player started with a word that began with an A, the second player should start their line with a word that begins with the letter B.

#4: This pattern will continue all the way through the scene until all letters in the alphabet have been used to start a line of dialogue.

#5: The rule that separates this game from a regular Alphabet Scene is that the first word of each line has to be something 'evil'. You can be loose with your interpretation as to what counts as evil.

#6: The Emcee can interject and make a player try a line again if they don't feel the player started the line with a word that was evil, or that was evil enough. This creates a game within the game where the players have to keep the evil level suitably high with these words.

#7: It's worth keeping in mind that the whole scene doesn't have to be evil, just the opening word of each line. This can create opportunities for fun in that other than the opening word of each line, the scene itself could be quite nice or sweet. How you incorporate the evil words are up to you.

How Does the Game End?

Once the performers have gone all the way through the alphabet.

Here is an example of how the game could flow:

Player 1: *Arson…al are my favourite soccer team.*

Player 2: *Boil the kettle, will you? And we'll watch the match.*

Player 1: *Crucify Manchester United. That's what I want them to do.*

Player 2: *Damnation. You know I support Man United.*

Player 1: *Evil…ution of the sport has meant that United are not as good as they used to be.*

Player 2: *Farted. They farted away their success long ago.*

As you can see from this example, you can use the evil words literally, or you can use them as part of a longer word that in its own right may not be seen as evil.

'Boil' may be questioned as to how that could count as evil, but this could be justified as referring to the lump or wart that someone may want removed.

Pro Tips:

Pro Tip #1: I would recommend that you really hit that first word to make it clear what you have said. Giving each starting word a sense of evil will help make the audience understand as to how it could be considered as such.

Pro Tip #2: If the Emcee doesn't feel a word is evil enough, there is room for them to interject and ask how a word is justified as evil. The Emcee could call *'freeze'* or just interject. If they do interject, I would suggest that the performers in the scene take a brief moment to respond out of character as themselves to give any justification. As soon as this is given and the Emcee accepts the justification, be ready to jump straight back into character and continue the scene.

Pro Tip #3: A player could have fun choosing a word that is very obviously not something evil, but saying it ironically. Doing this would imply it is something evil just because it was said in the game. An example of this may be to say *Disney* for the letter D, or the name of a celebrity or politician.

Everyone is raven about the evil alphabet game

39: THE EVIL PHONETIC ALPHABET SCENE

Emcee Intro Script: Our next game is one of our most challenging and devious improv games for our performers. We are going to play the Evil Phonetic Alphabet Game. If you're familiar with the NATO phonetic alphabet, you'll know that there are words that represent each letter. Alpha is A, Bravo is B, Charlie is C, Delta is D, and so on. Each word is distinct, and it is obvious what letter each word refers to.

For this game, we have devised a new phonetic alphabet where it is not obvious what letter the words refer to.

For example, the letter A is represented by the word *'aye'*. This is spelled A-Y-E as in *'aye aye captain'*. The letter B is represented by the word *'Bdelloid'* which has a silent B at the start. Cue starts with a C, but sounds like it begins with an Q. You'll see how this game unfolds as our performers play it.

Challenge Style: Scene based

Players: 2

Ask the Audience For: A skill you wish you were better at.

Setup: As the audience won't be familiar with this alphabet, it would be recommended to display the Evil Phonetic Alphabet during the game. This can either be on a projection, or on cue cards.

How to Play the Game:

#1: Two players create a scene.

#2: Every time a player starts a new line of dialogue, they will have to begin the sentence with the word that represents the next letter in the Evil Phonetic Alphabet. They will start with Aye and go all the way through the Evil Phonetic Alphabet until the final line is started with the word Zhivago.

#3: The aim is to use each of these words creatively. To attempt to make them fit naturally into the scene. Sometimes you'll be able to easily start a line with the word as is. Other times you may benefit from manipulating a word to sound like another word.

For example, if you take the word *'Heir'* which represents the letter H in the Evil Phonetic Alphabet, it is pronounced like the word *'air'* as in what people breath.

You could use the word to mean either heir or air, or you could find a variety of other ways to manipulate the usage. Examples of this would be to say *'heir loom'* or *'heir-ry legs'*. You can be as creative as you like to manipulate words but should always take care to ensure that the audience can understand what you intend to say.

How Does the Game End?

The game ends once the performers have gone all the way through the Evil Phonetic Alphabet.

The whole Evil Phonetic Alphabet goes as follows:

Aye *(sounds like I or Eye)*

Bdelloid *(sounds like Dell oid)*

Cue *(sounds like the letter Q)*

Double you *(sounds like the letter W)*

Eye *(sounds like the letter I)*

Fel *(sounds like you are saying Vel and is the Welsh word for Like)*

Gnome *(sounds like Nome)*

Heir *(sounds like Air)*

Irksome *(sounds like it starts with a U like urk some)*

Jesus *(sounds like Hey Zeus)*

Knight *(sounds like Night)*

Llanto *(said as Yanto and is the Spanish word for crying)*

Mnemonic *(sounds like Nemonic)*

Ngoni *(sounds like Goney and is a West African instrument)*

Ouija *(sounds like Wee Gee)*

Pneumonia *(sounds like New Monia)*

Quay *(sounds like Key)*

République *(pronounced with a French guttural R)*

Sea *(sounds like the letter C)*

Tsunami *(sounds like Sue Narmy)*

Urn *(sounds like Earn)*

Vamos *(said as Bamos and is the Spanish word for 'let's go')*

Wrong *(sounds like Rong)*

Xi *(sounds like the word Shee)*

You *(sounds like the letter U)*

Zhivago *(sounds like Shiv Argo)*

Pro Tips:

Pro Tip #1: Something you can really lean into with this game is the idea that the Emcee is giving a huge challenge to the performers. The game is called the *'Evil'* phonetic alphabet based on it being confusing and the words not sounding like they begin with the letters that they actually do.

Everyone in the scene should play into the idea that the Emcee is purposely trying to give an impossible challenge for the performers to complete. The Emcee could relish watching the performers struggle and play something of an antagonistic persona.

Pro Tip #2: This is a game where the performers have free reign to break character and express how challenging it is, or how confused they are. This of course, is just a persona, and should be done to comic effect.

Showing confusion or mispronouncing words are things you can do to highlight the absurdity of the challenge. The Emcee can also interject to correct performers who say the wrong thing or pronounce things incorrectly.

Pro Tip #3: I would suggest that you play this game only if the words from the Evil Phonetic Alphabet can be displayed to the audience during the game.

You could read it to them before the game starts, but even if you do this, having a visual reminder during the game is essential to the audience appreciating the challenge.

Pro Tip #4: If the performers are able to learn the Evil Phonetic Alphabet, they will be able to be more fluent in this game. It will also give them a weird party trick as they'll be among the first in the world to know this new alphabet.

However, even if you do learn the Evil Phonetic Alphabet, it may be worth playing dumb as if you don't know it. This is because the audience will relate more to you not knowing it than if you show off that you do know it. This said, it could be fun for one player to act like they know it well, and the other to be baffled by the strange new alphabet.

See Also: In the first Extreme Improv Big Book of Improv Games, I detailed one of my Extreme Improv original games which is known as the NATO Phonetic Alphabet Game. The Evil Phonetic Alphabet Game would make a good companion game played after the NATO version. How the two games are played is very similar but for their use of different alphabets.

Reading up on that one will certainly give insight in how to play this game. Within this book there is also the game Elemental Madness, which like this game asks players to pronounce words creatively.

40: ELEMENTAL MADNESS

Emcee Intro Script: We're now going to play Elemental Madness, also known as the Periodic Table Game. Our performers are going to create a scene where each line of dialogue has to start with one of the words that represents one of the chemical elements from the periodic table.

But don't worry, we're not going to get too sciencey here. We want the words to be used creatively. For example, if a character said *'lead astray were you?'* or *'sulfar so good'*, you'll see how the words are being used creatively rather than literally.

One more thing to note is that both the characters in our scene happen to be called Dr. Ium, spelled *'I U M.'* The reason for this is because almost half of the words in the periodic table end in the suffix 'ium' and naming every character in the scene Ium helps things make a little bit more sense...You'll see what I mean once the scene begins.

Challenge Style: Scene based

Players: 2

Ask the Audience For: Something the two Iums are doing that isn't directly related to science.

How to Play the Game:

#1: Every time a performer starts a new line of dialogue, it has to begin with one of the words from the periodic table. For example:

Player 1: *Silly con we got ourselves tangled up in, wasn't it?*

Player 2: *Ahhhh, gone and reminded me of that again haven't you...*

Player 1: *Firm Ium. You have to stay firm in your convictions if we'll resolve this con.*

Player 2: *Holm Ium...you're a real Sherlock Holmes all at once, aren't you?*

Player 1: *Einstein Ium. I'd compare myself more to Albert Einstein...*

As seen in the example, players have taken Silicon, Argon, Fermium, Holmium and Einsteinium and turned them into other words.

#2: In addition to the words that represent each element, you can also start each line by pronouncing the chemical symbol. For example:

Player 1: *Bro, mine is frozen solid!*

Player 2: *Brrrrrrrr it is cold in here.*

Player 1: *Cd of music will help distract us.*

Player 2: *Y?*

Player 1: *Gold albums will encourage us to dance and keep warm.*

A combination of the names of chemical elements and the chemical symbols were both used. Both Bromine and Br were used, and these both relate to the same element. Br could be pronounced as *'Bee Are'* but was instead used as 'Brrrrr' with a rolling R to give a sense of cold.

The letter Y is used to represent Yttrium, and in the above example would have been pronounced as the word *'why'*.

#3: I would make a point to highlight that the characters in the scene are called Ium, which could be joked as a misspelling of the name Ian.

The reason for this is because of the one hundred and eighteen elements in the periodic table, around fifty of them end in the suffix 'ium'. It would be difficult to use many of the element names creatively if you always had to use the ending ium which itself doesn't really sound like many words in its own right. By making it the character's names, it means you can use dozens more of the elements with it just sounding like you are addressing the other character.

For example, Europium gives you the word Europe, Barium gives you the name Barry, and Rhodium gives you the word road. If we were to put these into some dialogue, it would mean the characters are saying the name Ium often, but actually will make the scene flow quite well.

For example:

Player 1: *Europe Ium. I want to go to Europe.*

Player 2: *Barry Ium. Go with Barry instead of me.*

Player 1: *Road Ium. Barry doesn't know which road to take.*

#4: I would suggest you really emphasise each element name or chemical symbol you say. You can't trust that your audience will really know their periodic table super well, so making it very clear will help them keep up. This will also give the players in the scene some extra thinking time, as I imagine that many performers may have to revise the periodic table in order to play this game well.

How Does the Game End?

When the players are starting to run out of different elements.

Pro Tips:

Pro Tip #1: Some of the elements are more common usage, such as Oxygen or Carbon. I would say it is ok to use them in either their standard, or creative ways. For example, you could say *'Carbon pencil is what I need to sign my name.'* Alternatively, you could say *'Car bon. It is a good French car.'* You could use both of those variations within one game, although I'd lean towards not reusing the same element repeatedly if you can avoid it.

Pro Tip #2: Although similar to Alphabet Scene games, this game isn't designed around using each of the elements in a specific order. Whilst you could choose to start the game with Hydrogen and work towards Oganesson in the order of their atomic number, my feeling is that this game will be challenging enough as it is, as not many people are as familiar with all 118 elements.

Additionally, you can also use the chemical symbols such as Ne and Ga in place of the element names, giving a total of 236 things to use, which is more than you would ever need to use in a single round of this game.

Pro Tip #3: Inexperienced players may muddle the rules of this game with those from a traditional Alphabet Scene. They may think you can use the chemical symbols in the same way as regular letters are used in an Alphabet Scene. For example, players may think of the element Carbon which has the chemical symbol 'C'. They then may think they can start a line with any word that begins with the letter C, such as *'cheese'* or *'cute'*. That would be a mistake. Very specifically, for this game to stay on track, there has to be strict limits to how chemical symbols can be used. In the case of Carbon, and its chemical symbol 'C', I would say that it should always be pronounced as in the word *'see'*.

Pro Tip #4: Feel free to use fictional elements like Adamantium, Dalekanium, Dilithium, Kryptonite, Vibranium and Improvanium.

Here is a full list of the elements and their chemical symbols from the periodic table. Feel free to write your ideas for how each word can be used or manipulated for the game next to each word.

1. Hydrogen (H)
2. Helium (He)
3. Lithium (Li)
4. Beryllium (Be)
5. Boron (B)
6. Carbon (C)
7. Nitrogen (N)
8. Oxygen (O)
9. Fluorine (F)
10. Neon (Ne)
11. Sodium (Na)
12. Magnesium (Mg)
13. Aluminum (Al)
14. Silicon (Si)
15. Phosphorus (P)
16. Sulfur (S)
17. Chlorine (Cl)
18. Argon (Ar)
19. Potassium (K)
20. Calcium (Ca)
21. Scandium (Sc)
22. Titanium (Ti)
23. Vanadium (V)
24. Chromium (Cr)
25. Manganese (Mn)
26. Iron (Fe)
27. Cobalt (Co)
28. Nickel (Ni)

29.Copper (Cu)

30.Zinc (Zn)

31.Gallium (Ga)

32.Germanium (Ge)

33.Arsenic (As)

34.Selenium (Se)

35.Bromine (Br)

36.Krypton (Kr)

37.Rubidium (Rb)

38.Strontium (Sr)

39.Yttrium (Y)

40.Zirconium (Zr)

41.Niobium (Nb)

42.Molybdenum (Mo)

43.Technetium (Tc)

44.Ruthenium (Ru)

45.Rhodium (Rh)

46.Palladium (Pd)

47.Silver (Ag)

48.Cadmium (Cd)

49.Indium (In)

50.Tin (Sn)

51.Antimony (Sb)

52.Tellurium (Te)

53.Iodine (I)

54.Xenon (Xe)

55.Cesium (Cs)

56.Barium (Ba)

57.Lanthanum (La)

58.Cerium (Ce)

59.Praseodymium (Pr)

60.Neodymium (Nd)

61.Promethium (Pm)

62.Samarium (Sm)

63.Europium (Eu)

64.Gadolinium (Gd)

65.Terbium (Tb)

66.Dysprosium (Dy)

67.Holmium (Ho)

68.Erbium (Er)

69.Thulium (Tm)

70.Ytterbium (Yb)

71.Lutetium (Lu)

72.Hafnium (Hf)

73.Tantalum (Ta)

74.Tungsten (W)

75.Rhenium (Re)

76.Osmium (Os)

77.Iridium (Ir)

78.Platinum (Pt)

79.Gold (Au)

80.Mercury (Hg)

81.Thallium (Tl)

82.Lead (Pb)

83.Bismuth (Bi)

84.Polonium (Po)

85.Astatine (At)

86.Radon (Rn)

87.Francium (Fr)

88.Radium (Ra)

89.Actinium (Ac)

90.Thorium (Th)

91.Protactinium (Pa)

92.Uranium (U)

93.Neptunium (Np)

94.Plutonium (Pu)

95.Americium (Am)

96.Curium (Cm)

97.Berkelium (Bk)

98.Californium (Cf)

99.Einsteinium (Es)

100.Fermium (Fm)

101.Mendelevium Md)

102. Nobelium (No)

103. Lawrencium (Lr)

104.Rutherfordium Rf)

105. Dubnium (Db)

106. Seaborgium (Sg)

107. Bohrium (Bh)

108. Hassium (Hs)

109. Meitnerium (Mt)

110.Darmstadtium(Ds)

111. Roentgenium (Rg)

112. Copernicium (Cn)

113. Nihonium (Nh)

114. Flerovium (Fl)

115. Moscovium (Mc)

116. Livermorium (Lv)

117. Tennessine (Ts)

118. Oganesson (Og)

SECTION 4: SPECIFIC ROLES/SCENARIOS

This section is all about games where there are set characters, locations or themes.

Oh nothing. Just an Emperor Penguin

41: IF OBJECTS COULD TALK

Emcee Intro Script: This improv challenge is called If Objects Could Talk and is a game where our performers will be playing talking sentient versions of objects and give us their view on the world.

Challenge Style: Scene based

Players: 2+

Ask the Audience For: A suggestion of types of objects that the performers will act as. This could be very specific, such as they are all loose cables in a drawer, or less specific like they are all kitchen appliances.

You could also ask for an important life event that the objects will be experiencing during the scene.

How to Play the Game:

#1: To have an idea of what this game aims for, it is useful to think about the film Toy Story, if you are familiar with it. In that film, it explores what the lives of toys would be like if they could secretly talk and walk around. In this game, the players will be performing as walking/talking versions of whatever kind of objects that the audience has suggested for them.

#2: In the early stages of the game, you should show off how you think you would talk and move about if you were the object you have been assigned as. If you weren't personally assigned a specific object, but the audience's suggestion was something more general like *'things you find in a tool kit'* you will have to make sure it is clear to the other performers and the audience what object you are.

For example, the simplest way to do this would be through dialogue such as *'They don't call me Phil the hammer for nothing'* and then proceed to hammer something with your head.

#3: The fun in the game comes from relating the object you are playing to everyday activities and human experiences. Here's a few examples that use a tool kit as the suggestion of objects for the scene.

A hammer may knock on a door with their head.

A saw may always say cutting remarks.

A level may always try to be the balanced character and keep everyone calm.

A screwdriver may move about the stage in a circular motion. They may also think others are being screwy with them.

How Does the Game End?

The game ends at the discretion of the Emcee.

Pro Tips:

Pro Tip #1: Make sure that you build a story throughout the scene. It can be easy to make the mistake of just focusing on coming up with ways to highlight how you are your object and lose a sense of any story.

Pro Tip #2: Some objects lend themselves to a certain style of movement, such as a ball bouncing around the stage, or scissors being about to walk around because the blades could be legs.

If you're struggling to think how you may move as your object, you can always imagine your object in a very cartoonish way. It may be that you are a pair of scissors with cartoon arms and legs out the sides and googly eyes.

The game is more about taking on the personality and world view of the object than you being restricted to how that object may be able to move in the real world.

42: WEIRD NEWSCASTERS

Emcee Intro Script: It's time for Weird Newscasters! Our cast will be taking on the role of the news readers from television. One of them will be the Lead Anchor, another will be the Co-Anchor, another will be the Weather Reporter, and another will be the Sports Reporter. Each character will have an unusual quirk which will influence how they present their segment of the news.

Challenge Style: Scene based

Players: 2-4

Setup: Players could stand or sit for this game, with the Anchor and Co-Anchor usually sat directly facing the audience, and the other presenters stood either side.

Ask the Audience For: Optional. You could ask the audience for what their individual quirks are, or the Emcee could just assign what each player's quirk is instead of asking for suggestions.

The Lead Anchor is typically in the role of a comedic straight man, without a quirk. This lets them react to the others and keep things in order without everyone being something over the top and silly.

The quirks can be anything really but should be something that will affect the way they present the news. Examples may be that they're sad everyone has forgotten their birthday, they are really an alien, they are a retired war veteran who keeps having flashbacks to the war or that they have hiccups.

How to Play the Game:

#1: The Lead Anchor will start things off by welcoming the viewing audience to the show and maybe introducing one or two headlines of the day. These can still be funny, but this character will be the "normal" strait laced character.

#2: The Lead Anchor will then hand over to their Co-Anchor who will report on another story or two. As they do it, they will do it affected by whatever their quirk is.

#3: The Lead Anchor will then hand things over to the Weather Reporter and we'll see their presentation affected by their quirk. After this, the Lead Anchor will hand things over to the Sports Reporter.

How Does the Game End?

After the final player doing weather or sports has finished their segment, the Lead Anchor should do a short ending to wrap up the news programme.

Pro Tips:

Pro Tip #1: If you are playing a newscaster with a quirk, remember that you still need to deliver the news as well as demonstrate your quirk. Your quirk should just be incidental to you saying the news, and not in place of it.

Pro Tip #2: This game has a definite structure, and this is something you will get through practice. Whilst there is room for other players to speak outside of their news segment, this should ideally follow the structure and not become a free-for-all.

Pro Tip #3: Each news segment could last as little as twenty to thirty seconds. I wouldn't expect them to last any longer than this.

43: MIDWIFE CRISIS

Emcee Intro Script: Our next game is called Midwife Crisis! One of our performers will play a character who is about to give birth. Unfortunately, they haven't made it to the hospital in time, and they're going to have to rely on the kindness of strangers to help deliver this baby!

Challenge Style: Scene based

Players: 3

Ask the Audience For: A suggestion of where the mother to be is when the labour begins.

Also get a suggestion of who is at this location that is going to have to help deliver the baby. This could be someone specific like Queen Victoria, or a more general suggestion, like a plumber.

How to Play the Game:

#1: The opening of the scene should be to establish who the characters are and where the scene is taking place.

One player should take on the role of the expectant Mother. Who the other characters are is up to you.

One of the other characters could be the father or someone who knows the Mother. Alternatively, the other two characters could both be people who are strangers to the Mother.

#2: After about thirty seconds to one minute, the Mother should start to show signs that they are in labour.

#3: Based on what the location/scenario is, it may be obvious what the challenges will be for the Mother to reach a hospital or midwife before the birth. If the challenges aren't obvious, the players should create a situation which puts up barriers to the birth going smoothly.

#4: The character who isn't the mother/father should start to get more involved *(especially if they've not been introduced into the scene* *yet)*. They should assist trying to get the Mother to be to the hospital, make her more comfortable, or actually assist with delivering the baby.

How Does the Game End?

The game should ideally end with the birth of the baby and maybe a short period of time after this to see the characters reactions.

Pro Tips:

Pro Tip #1: I wouldn't suggest that the characters who are strangers to the Mother are midwives or doctors, as the potential for humour comes from them not knowing how to help.

Pro Tip #2: You could have characters who think they can help when really, they can't.

For example, an overconfident office manager who feels they can handle high pressure situations or a butcher who thinks it'll just be like removing giblets from a chicken.

The Time Travelling Midwife always delivers on time

44: ROBOTS

Emcee Intro Script: It's time to play Robots. Our performers are going to be playing a day in the life of robots. They will behave like robots, and they will speak like robots, using robot language.

Challenge Style: Scene based

Players: 2+

Ask the Audience For: An everyday activity or problem that regular families or colleagues face.

How to Play the Game:

#1: There are a few ways to approach this, but ideally, you should all agree in rehearsal how the robots can communicate.

Is it that everyone does stiff emotionless voices like was stereotyped in robots during 1950s and 1960s sci-fi TV shows? Do they speak in binary code where they can only say 0s and 1s? Or do they speak just like regular human beings but replace everyday terms and expressions with robotised language?

For example:

Human language: *I'm so tired. I need to get some sleep.*

Robot version: *My processor is overheating. I need to power down.*

Human language: *I saw you looking at Stacy earlier. Are you cheating on me and planning to break up?*

Robot version: *I observed you observing the new model earlier. Are you interfacing with her and planning to upgrade?*

You could all do the same, or you could do a combination of these approaches.

#2: Think about your physicality. Robots are portrayed as being efficient and precise in their movements usually, so you could lean into this.

#3: Building off the example language in step one, think about what a robot's world view, values and priorities would be. Are they concerned with their children passing exams? Are they programmed to take over the earth? Do they have a God? Maybe they pray to Apple or Microsoft. You can have fun inventing an alternative robot version of everything humans normally have.

How Does the Game End?

The scene can end whenever the Emcee feels the story has reached a good end point. This could be after a big laugh from the audience, or some kind of revelation in the story, or a cliffhanger.

Pro Tips:

Pro Tip #1: A fun approach to this game is to show that robots still have all the same issues and daily problems that humans do but handle them differently. If a character is sad because someone had died, maybe they add the sad memory files to the recycle bin or stuff like that.

Pro Tip #2: Robots may have to deal with challenges that humans don't. Things like rust, water damage, run out of memory etc.

45: JUST ADD ZOMBIES

Emcee Intro Script: We're now going to play the game known as Just Add Zombies. The scene is for multiple players, and the way it works is thus…We will join the characters on an average day, but after about a minute, the scene will be invaded by more performers who will take on the role of zombies. We'll then see how the scene unfolds and continues with the presence of the zombies.

Challenge Style: Scene based

Players: 3+

Ask the Audience For: Where the scene is set. This could be a specific type of event, like at a wedding or a birthday party. Alternatively, it could be based on a movie, or well-known story. The choice is the audiences, for wherever they would like to see zombies added to.

How to Play the Game:

#1: When the scene begins, the players will want to establish the scenario as it is before the arrival of the zombies.

#2: After about a minute, other players should enter the scene as people who have been bitten and are about to turn into zombies, or as already fully formed zombies.

#3: The scene should continue with the characters both trying to survive the zombies, but also still trying to do or achieve whatever the scenario was before the arrival of the zombies. For example, if the scene was about a wedding, you could have fun with the father of the bride insisting the wedding go ahead as they've already paid for the reception party.

How Does the Game End?

The game should end with either the zombies killing the main characters, or vice versa.

Pro Tips:

Pro Tip #1: You could have fun with foreshadowing the arrival of the zombies. Characters could mention seeing people biting others, or maybe one of the main characters has been bitten already.

Pro Tip #2: Characters could also be somewhat oblivious to the arrival of the zombies, and it take some time for the penny to drop.

Variations: This game could also be played as Just Add Aliens, Just Add Pirates, or Just Add Llamas...you get the idea! Feel free to ask the audience for what group of individuals will invade the scene.

Read the tips to get a head in this game

46: KING OF THE JUNGLE

Emcee Intro Script: Let's play King of the Jungle! In this scene, the performers are going to take on the roles in the hierarchy of animals.

They'll be playing the likes of lions, tigers and bears, cats, dogs and mice, and so on and so forth. And then we'll see how these animals deal with human like situations like running a government, or a big business or even the dynamics of a royal family.

Challenge Style: Scene based

Players: 3-5

Ask the Audience For: Problems that the real-world governments, businesses or royal families may have to deal with.

You also have the option of asking the audience what animal each performer is playing.

How to Play the Game:

#1: The performers act as anthropomorphic animals. This means they act as animals that behave in human like ways. Therefore, they can talk, and mostly behave like humans, but incorporate animal like behaviours and references into what they do.

#2: The performers then show off the dynamics between the different animals, and how their animal type would tackle solving the issues in the scenario.

How Does the Game End?

The game ends when the Emcee feels the story has reached a crescendo.

Pro Tips:

Pro Tip #1: This game is an opportunity to connect animal behaviour to aspects of real-world human relations and conflict. Some animals may just want to eat their rival whereas humans don't do that. You can have fun drawing parallels between the likes of female lions doing a lot of the hunting, whilst the men lay about, female black widow spiders being dominant and eating their husbands, or dogs recognising each other by smell.

Pro Tip #2: Play with and find the balance between human and animal qualities. How does the animal you are playing walk? How do they sound when they talk?

The aim is that your animal characters will talk like humans, but you may find the right opportunity for them to make animal sounds if they are excited or emotional.

47: THE REASON WE CAN'T GO OUTSIDE

Emcee Intro Script: In our next game, we'll be exploring the Reason We Can't Go Outside!!! Audience, you'll suggest whatever that reason is, and then we'll see how the characters cope with whatever it is on the outside world.

Challenge Style: Scene based

Players: 2+

Ask the Audience For: What the reason the characters can't go outside is.

How to Play the Game:

#1: The scene should unfold with the characters either having just discovered the reason they cannot go outside, or that they have been stuck inside for a long while by the time the scene begins. This will affect their attitude to the circumstances that prevent them from going outside.

#2: The object of the game is for the characters to not go outside. No matter what. It's up to the performers to emphasise to the audience the risks and dangers posed by whatever the reason is that they don't go outside.

So, even though the scene is about not going outside, the debate and question of if any characters ever could or should go outside should continually come up in the scene.

#3: The focus on the scene should also be about whatever the characters are trying to do whilst inside. This could be something they need to do to survive or something they have to get done before they ever could go outside. You'll need to find the balance between the characters focussing on what is going on inside, and their fear or desire to explore what is outside.

How Does the Game End?

The game ends either when a character finally does go outside, or when the Emcee feels the scene has reached a good end point.

If a character ever does outside, the scene should not continue with the characters showing the audience what is outside. The scene should always remain set on the inside.

Pro Tips:

Pro Tip #1: You can play with the idea of characters feeling trapped or desperate to go outside, and others needing to convince them to stay inside or prevent them from going outside.

Pro Tip #2: Think about how your character feels about the person they are trapped inside with. This scene will be as much about the dynamic between the characters as anything else to do with the tasks they are trying to achieve or the risks of the outside world.

Beware if you go outside, you could meet mythological creatures like the Basilisk, Baku or Gastro Nemesis

48: BLACKOUT

Emcee Intro Script: We're now going to play Blackout! In this game our performers are going to create a scene. After about thirty seconds into the scene, there will be a total blackout in whatever location the scene is set in.

Don't worry audience, we won't be switching off the lights. We want you to see how our characters would react if they were in a situation where they were alone in the dark...

Challenge Style: Scene based

Players: 2+

Ask the Audience For: A specific location like a hospital or school, or an activity that the performers are attempting to do.

How to Play the Game:

#1: The players start the scene normally, just so we can get a sense of who the characters are and what they are doing in the scenario.

#2: After thirty seconds the Emcee shouts *'blackout'* and the performers in the scene have to react as if the lights have suddenly gone out.

#3: The remainder of the scene should be about the characters trying to manage in the dark, and we'll see if they attempt to continue whatever it was they were doing before the lights went out.

How Does the Game End?

When the Emcee is ready for the scene to end, they should shout *'Lights on!'* We could then see a few seconds of the characters reacting to having the lights on before the Emcee truly ends it.

Pro Tips:

Pro Tip #1: The fun of this game is seeing how people would behave in the pitch black if we could still see them. Things you can do is pull funny expressions like having wide eyes as if you're trying really hard to see in the dark.

You can also take baby steps and have your arms stretched out to feel your way around because you are worried you may bump into something or someone.

Pro Tip #2: You can also have fun with characters doing sneaky things in the dark because they know the other characters cannot see them. This can include making rude gestures right in front of people or moving or stealing things, or hitting into someone and pretending it was an accident.

Of course, it is worth saying that the performers in the game should always maintain respect for one another, and this game shouldn't be used as an excuse to invade another person's personal space. This is something you should discuss with the players before they play this game together.

SECTION 5: EMCEE INTERJECT SCENES

The following batch of games are all ones where the Emcee may occasionally interject during the course of the scene to give some new instructions.

Inject a little interjection into the games

49: TRAFFIC LIGHTS

Emcee Intro Script: We are now going to play Traffic Lights! In this game, I *(the Emcee)* will call out Red Light, Amber Light and Green Light to increase, decrease or normalise the speed and intensity of the scene.

Challenge Style: Scene based

Players: 2+

Ask the Audience For: Things that scare you.

How to Play the Game:

#1: The players begin a scene to establish the scenario and characters.

#2: At any point the Emcee can call out the following phrases to affect the scene in different ways.

Red Light: Calling this out will dramatically halt the intensity of the action.

Amber Light: Will normalise the intensity of the action.

Green Light: Will cause the action to speed up and get bigger and more intense.

#3: To clarify what the light system controls, it isn't just speed, but the momentum and passion, the emotion and the stakes of the scene.

If left on Green, the scene will continue to build momentum to become increasingly more high stakes. Calling Red Light will stop the action in its tracks, and in turn will be world stopping for the characters. A Red Light may make characters lethargic, slow and without ambition.

An Amber Light will set things normal again. People will see things with more clarity and not rush into things like a mad bull as they would with a Green Light.

The meaning of each of the lights can be interpreted in different ways, but shouldn't just be about the pace of the scene or speed of speech.

How Does the Game End?

When the Emcee calls time on it with a final Red Light.

Pro Tips:

Pro Tip #1: If Green Light is called, don't just take things instantly as far as they can go. Build things up bit by bit.

A Red Light should be a fairly rapid decline in intensity but doesn't have to be instantaneous. An Amber Light should quickly take things back to neutral.

Pro Tip #2: Something you can experiment with in rehearsals is the idea that the Emcee can call different lights to individual players. For example, *'Steve Green Light'* and then only Steve is in Green Light mode whilst the other players are doing either Red or Amber. This will be harder for the audience to keep track of so I would suggest using this idea sparingly, but may be fun once or twice in a game.

50: RHYMING CHOICES

Emcee Intro Script: We're going to play a game of Rhyming Choices. The performers will create a scene, but every so often I *(The Emcee)* will call out *'Rhyme that choice'*. When I do this, whatever the last thing the performer who just spoke said will be erased from the script. They'll have to replace their old choice with a new choice that rhymes with their old choice...

See Also: In the original Extreme Improv Big Book of Improv Games, we cover the game Extreme Choices. If you want to delve deeper into how to play this game, I'd recommend referring to that also.

Challenge Style: Scene based

Players: 2+

Ask the Audience For: An activity

How to Play the Game:

#1: Two players start the scene and establish the characters and story.

#2: At any point the Emcee can call out the phrase *'Rhyme that choice.'* If they do this, whatever the last line of dialogue was, it is effectively scrubbed and erased from the "script".

The Player who last spoke will have to then create a new choice of line of dialogue that rhymes with the one that was just erased. For example:

Player 1*: I think we should head to the shop.*

Emcee: *Rhyme that choice!*

Player 1: *We'd better run, here comes a cop!*

Player 2: *Oh no you're right! It's the fuzz!*

Emcee: *Rhyme that choice!*

Player 2: *Darn it, they're really ruining my buzz.*

Player 1: *Quick let's hide behind this dumpster.*

Player 2: *I don't want to sit next to a trash can!*

Emcee: *Rhyme that choice!*

Player 2: *No, lets run! We need to dash man!*

As you'll see from the example given, the Emcee doesn't have to interject after every line. In fact, I'd say the Emcee definitely shouldn't interject so much that the scene can't build momentum.

The Emcee can also choose not to interject when the players and audience may expect it.

#3: The Emcee can also keep interjecting and calling *'Rhyme that choice'* to the same player multiple times before they let the scene continue. As the scene does continue, the Emcee can increase the frequency of how many times they get the characters to rhyme their choices.

How Does the Game End?

When the Emcee feels it has run its course.

Pro Tips:

Pro Tip #1: Remember that the new line should replace the old one, and not just build upon or continue it.

Pro Tip #2: If you can't think of a rhyme, don't shy away from it. There's a bunch of ways it can be handled. If you take it slow, the audience may know you can't think of a rhyme and will probably be forgiving if your rhyme is weak or wrong.

Another option is that the other player may see that you're struggling and be able to interject with a rhyme for you.

If all else fails, just use the same word or make up a nonsense word to rhyme. The audience will probably let you get away with this tactic once or twice. If you make it obvious through your facial expression or tone of voice that you're trying to get away with something that you know is wrong, you're more likely to win them over.

51: EMOTIONAL LEVELS

Emcee Intro Script: It's time to check our Emotional Levels! In this game, as the performers do their scene, I *(the Emcee)* will point to a performer and call out numbers from one to ten. When I do this, I would like the performer to elevate or lower their emotional level to that number on a one to ten scale. I may also simply call out *'more'* or *'less'* and the actor will have to respond accordingly.

Challenge Style: Scene based

Players: 2+

Ask the Audience For: Something you do with a friend

How to Play the Game:

#1: The game starts, and the performers start acting out the scene to establish the characters and their relationship to one another.

#2: At various points, the Emcee can interject to call out a number from one to ten whilst pointing at one of the performers. That performer will have to adjust the level of emotion they are demonstrating in the scene to reflect that number on a one to ten scale.

#3: The Emcee can also call out 'more' or 'less' to a performer whilst pointing at them to get them to increase their emotional level.

How Does the Game End?

The game ends when the Emcee says so...

Pro Tips:

Pro Tip #1: Do what you can to demonstrate the various levels of emotion as different from one another. If you are showing sadness, or love, for example, a seven shouldn't be the same as a six. A ten should be the most you can possibly show, and a one should be the minimum.

Pro Tip #2: Performers, you don't have to stay in just one emotion. If you say you love the other character and they reject you, and you were showing level ten emotion, that will now go from level ten love to level ten rejection or despair.

From chill to thrill to ill in four stages

52: THE EMOTION POLICE

Emcee Intro Script: With the rise in artificial intelligence, computers are becoming ever more human like. But likewise, it can be said that humans are becoming more machine like. We show less and less emotion and human connection every year.

In our next game, we'll explore this a little, as every so often we're going to jump forward in time. Every time we jump forward, we're going to ban another emotion from being used. If anyone uses a banned emotion, they will be removed from the scene by the Anti Emotion Police Control Force.

Challenge Style: Scene based

Players: 4+

Ask the Audience For: A place of work.

How to Play the Game:

#1: The scene will start off as a normal scene. Players should use the opening thirty seconds or minute to establish who the characters are and demonstrate lots of different emotions.

#2: Within the first minute, the Emcee should call *'Freeze'* and announce an emotion which the people of this world are now banned from showing publicly. The Emcee can either choose what emotion is banned based on what is happening in the scene, or they can ask the audience for a suggestion of a random emotion.

#3: The Emcee should also call that the scene has skipped forward some period of time. This could be a week, or a few months. The scene will then continue, and we'll then see how the characters are living their lives now that they have had time to adjust to not using the banned emotion.

#4: After another thirty to sixty seconds, the process should repeat, and another emotion gets banned.

#5: This process can repeat as many times as you want until many or all emotions are banned. As the scene goes further, you can speed up how often you ban extra emotions. You can also ban multiple emotions at once. If banning multiple at once, be aware that it will be harder for both the audience and the performers to keep track of what is banned or not.

How Does the Game End?

The game ends when the Emcee judges it should end.

Optional Elimination Based Variation

This version should start with several people in the scene. If someone shows a banned emotion – either by accident or as an act of rebellion, the Emcee can freeze the action and call in the Anti Emotion Police Control Force to take that individual away.

With this element, you can play the game as an elimination game where it keeps going until all but one player has been eliminated.

As a heads up, this wouldn't be a real competitive game, and players would have to purposely get themselves eliminated for entertainment purposes. The reason for this is because I expect it would be too easy to just not show banned emotions.

Pro Tips:

Pro Tip #1: Feel free to have fun with the rules of this game. One character could purposely attempt to evoke an emotional response from another character in order to get them taken away by the police.

Pro Tip #2: You can also have fun with characters talking in a blank and emotionless way. For example, if there is something that makes a character feel very angry, but anger is a banned emotion, they could say how cross they are in a very neutral way, or be clearly trying to suppress the emotion for fear of being taken away by the police.

53: FORWARD REVERSE

Emcee Intro Script: An improv favourite, our next game is Forward Reverse! As the players perform the scene, I *(the Emcee)* can call out terms like Forward, or Reverse, Pause, Mute, or Skip Chapter.

Basically, any of the buttons you may find on a remote control for the likes of a TV, video or DVD player, or on the likes of a Betamax, Blu Ray or Lazer Disc player. The players will then have to fast forward, or rewind their scene, or do whatever the instructions seem to indicate.

Challenge Style: Scene based

Players: 2+

Ask the Audience For: A theme for the scene

How to Play the Game:

#1: Players should start a normal scene. They will need to pay careful attention to anything they say, or do as they are likely to need to repeat these several times throughout the game. They will need to remember the order of any lines of dialogue or actions that happen.

#2: At any point, the Emcee can call out instructions to the performers that will dictate the order and speed of the scene, as well as other aspects of it. Here is a breakdown of what the different instructions could be and the effect they would each have:

Reverse: Say all the lines from the scene in reverse order. For clarity, you don't change the order of the words in the lines, and instead just change the order of the lines themselves.

So, if you said the line *'I love you'*, it would be repeated as *'I love you'* and not as *'you love I'*.

Forwards: The players should continue the scene going forwards and add new lines to the scene. If you have already been reversed in the scene, you should just repeat the lines in the forwards order before moving on to inventing new lines.

Fast Forwards: Same as forwards, but everything is said faster.

Mute: Continue the scene in mime. As a note with this, you should have a sense of what you are saying whilst muted so that you can say it out loud if not muted.

Skip Chapter: If this is called you should jump to a later point in the story. The Emcee can call to skip a chapter forward or backwards.

Swap Language: Can be called to change the dubbing of the scene into another language. If you know words from another language you could use these, or you can just speak in gibberish.

How Does the Game End?

When the Emcee thinks the scene has been played back and forth enough times.

Pro Tips:

Pro Tip #1: Try to keep lines short and manageable. If you start saying monologue length lines, you'll get stuck having to repeat huge amounts over and over.

Pro Tip #2: Make sure you include physical action as well as dialogue. These should also be repeated along with any dialogue.

54: CHARACTER SWAP

Emcee Intro Script: Character Swap! In this next improv challenge, at any time in the scene I *(the Emcee)* can call out *'swap!'* When I do this, the two performers involved in the scene will have to swap what character they are playing with the other performer.

Challenge Style: Scene based

Players: 2

Ask the Audience For: A type of relationship between two people.

How to Play the Game:

#1: For clarity of describing this game, I'll describe the two performers as Bob and Charlie. When the players have swapped roles, I'll refer to them as SwappedBob and SwappedCharlie.

#2: Bob and Charlie start the scene and should clearly establish their characters. I would suggest that the performers make strong choices with their characters, so they are clearly defined from one another in how they speak, how they move, and what their personalities are like.

#2: At any point, the Emcee can call out the word *'swap'* and the performers in the scene will have to swap the characters that they are playing.

#3: I would suggest that the scene is left to run for a good forty-five seconds before the performers start swapping characters with one another. This will give enough time for the performers to observe each other and see what it is they will need to emulate in order to play the other performer's character.

#4: The longer the scene goes on, the more frequently the Emcee can get the performers to swap roles.

How Does the Game End?

When the Emcee has swapped the characters back and forth several times.

Pro Tips:

Pro Tip #1: Even though both performers will be playing both characters, I would suggest that Bob and Charlie view the characters they start as, as their main character. The fun of the scene is in seeing how Bob plays SwappedCharlie, and how Charlie played SwappedBob. The audience will want to see the performer's version of the role they didn't create.

If you leave them swapped for too long, the character will end up becoming more influenced by the second performer to play the role rather than the original.

Pro Tip #2: There is a duality to how you play the characters in this game. Player 1/Bob can have fun by making SwappedCharlie do things that Player 2/Charlie may not have wanted Charlie to do in the scene. When Charlie is playing Charlie again, they will now have to deal with the consequences of whatever SwappedCharlie did.

This is your opportunity to take control of the character you weren't originally playing. You can make them do things that the performer who originated the role may not want their character to do.

Say you were Charlie, and the Emcee calls 'swap' and now you are SwappedBob. You could make SwappedBob give away all their money to Charlie, declare their eternal love or bow down and worship Charlie. The fun of the duality is that the audience will still identify your original character with 'being you' more than just your character.

SECTION 6: TURN TAKE STUFF

Games where players will take turns at specific tasks. Some of these games are best used as intro or outro games during shows. Others lend themselves well to competitive games or situations where you need to tie break things or pick a winner.

You'll pay for this!

OK. I'll send you a cheque mate

55: GEEK BATTLE

Emcee Intro Script: It's time for a Geek Battle! Two players will step forward and give their arguments to defend a movie, video game, TV show, or a character, and state why it is better than the one being defended by their opponent.

Here's the catch...our audience will decide what movie or character *(etc)* that they have to defend. Even if the player prefers the thing being defended by their opponent, they will have to do their best to win the debate.

Challenge Style: Turn take/Debate

Players: 2

Ask the Audience For: Either two movies, TV shows, characters from fiction, video games, books, songs, comic books or anything else like this.

Note: For ease of discussion, for the rest of the description, I'll assume that what is being debated is a movie.

How to Play the Game:

#1: Each player should be timed and given either thirty seconds or one minute to make their argument for the movie they are defending. They need to give the best argument for why it is better.

#2: After the first player has had their turn, the second player should be invited to give their rebuttal and defend why what they're defending is the better one. They will have the same length of time to do so.

How Does the Game End?

Once both players have given their arguments, the audience should be asked to vote on who made the better argument. The Emcee should make it clear that the vote is about which performer gave the better argument, and isn't based on which movie the audience prefer.

Once the vote has happened *(usually by cheering)* the winner should be announced.

Pro Tips:

Pro Tip #1: Remember to talk about both the movie you are defending as well as the movie your opponent is defending. It can be easy to just talk about one or the other and forget that the aim is to create an argument that compares both movies to one another.

Pro Tip #2: The Emcee can check with the players to make sure they know the movie they are defending, but I would be inclined to say that even if they don't know what the movie in question is, they should still have to talk about it.

If you don't know it well, just work with the limited details that you do know and do your best.

Pro Tip #3: If you know nothing at all about one or both movies, you can lean into that by saying that the other person's movie is so bad that you've never even heard of it. Or you can say that the other person's movie is so bad that your own is better even though you've never seen it.

Pro Tip #4: Even if you are a super fan of the thing you are defending you should keep in mind that not everyone in the audience will know all the different movies as well as others. So, whilst you could go super nerdy and give amazing observations that would do well at Comic Con, do keep in mind that you want to entertain everyone in the audience and not just a couple of super geeks.

56: DOUBLE IMPRESSION

Emcee Intro Script: We're about to play a game where the performers will have to do impressions. But…they will have to do an impression of one well-known person or character doing an impression of another well-known person or character. It's Double Impression time!

Challenge Style: Monologue

Players: 1+

Ask the Audience For: Two characters from fiction or people from history (or mix and match)

How to Play the Game:

#1: Let's say the audience give the suggestion of Andre the Giant doing an impression of Pinocchio.

You should attempt to do an impression of Andre the Giant as your main impression or base character. You'll then want to layer on top of this what you think Andre the Giant's impression of Pinocchio would be like. Pinocchio is therefore your secondary character.

#2: You have the choice whether you go straight into both impressions at once, or if you want to start off as the base character and then add the second character on top.

Using the Andre/Pinocchio example again, even if you can do a brilliant Pinocchio impression, we shouldn't ever see that on its own. Unless, of course, you are saying that Andre the Giant is able to do a fantastic impression of Pinocchio. The point is that we should see your impression of Andre doing an impression of Pinocchio. Not your impression of just Pinocchio.

So even if you can do a great Pinocchio, you may have to purposely sabotage it, in the quest of making it seem like its being done by Andre the Giant.

How Does the Game End?

If played as a solo performer game, the performer could indicate that they've finished their impression (usually with a bow) or the Emcee can cut them off. If done as a two or more player game, the Emcee should end the game with a vote on who the audience felt did the best.

Pro Tips:

Pro Tip #1: Remember, it's your base character doing an impression of your secondary character and not the other way around. So, if the audience ask for Andre doing an impression of Pinocchio, don't do Pinocchio doing an impression of Andre.

Pro Tip #2: Break the previous rule if you want. If you think you could do better by swapping the characters, then do that. But if you do this, only do so to get a laugh to help make it a better show.

If you do this, I'd always say that either you yourself, or the Emcee should acknowledge that you've done it back to front. Then I'd expect the Emcee to tell you to try again and do it the right way around or jokingly disqualify you for being sneaky or cheating.

57: NEXT TIME ON

Emcee Intro Script: Just before we wrap up the show today, we have just enough time for a preview of how our adventures will continue for our next show...

Challenge Style: Chain game

Players: 2+

Ask the Audience For: Audience don't make suggestions for this game.

How to Play the Game:

#1: After the Emcee has introduced the game, they should hand over to one of the performers. Let's say they hand over to Player 1.

#2: Player 1 will then say something that the audience can look forward to in the next show. This shouldn't be an actual preview of your next improv show and will instead be a tease of a storyline.

The idea for these teases is to emulate the kind of *'next time on'* segments that happen at the end of episodic TV shows. These teases aren't expected to be followed up on in the next show. They also don't actually have to relate to anything that has happened in the current show in progress.

For example:

Player 1: *In next week's show, we'll find out the dramatic truth about the real father of Kim's baby, and how that affects Meredith's inheritance. What are you looking forward to Player 2?*

Player 2: *Well, I'll be keeping a close eye on my business rivals, who I expect an explosive showdown with. Isn't that right Player 3?*

Player 3: *Be careful, cause I hear they're out for blood. Also, in next week's show we can expect the return of Next Door Brenda who we saw in one of the earlier sketches from tonight's show. Also a special appearance by our musical act Tony and the Tone Deafs.*

#3: As you'll see from the example I just gave, after each player has given their preview for what is happening on next week's show, they should specify which player they are handing over to next.

None of these storylines are likely to be followed up on. These are just for fun, and they either could relate to something seen in the show that you are just wrapping up, or they could be invented on the spot during this game.

How Does the Game End?

Once all players have given their previews of the next show. The final player to speak could wrap up the show in total, or they could hand things back over to the Emcee to officially wrap the show up.

Pro Tips:

Pro Tip #1: The player speaking should show real interest in what they are previewing. This will make the preview sound dramatic and enticing for the audience to want to see how the stories will develop.

Pro Tip #2: Players who are currently speaking could step into centre stage to do so, or they could step forward from wherever they are on stage. In both instances, but especially the latter, the other players should look to the current speaker to make sure there is focus on them.

58: WHAT I LEARNED TODAY

Emcee Intro Script: Before we wrap things up, each of the performers will give you a thought that you can take away from our show today. Hopefully it'll be something we can all learn from, to grow and be better people.

Challenge Style: Chain game

Players: 2+

Ask the Audience For: Not needed for this game.

How to Play the Game:

#1: After the Emcee introduces the round, they will hand things over to each player to give their thought.

#2: The idea of this game is that each player will give a thought of something they have learned from what has happened during the show. These could relate to things the characters did in the scenes, or it could be something the player has learned as a performer working on the show.

Here are some examples:

Player 1: *I've learned never to leave the window open during a tornado.*

Player 2: *My biggest take away from today's escapades is that it's important to look after your teaching assistant, even if they secretly hate you.*

Player 3: *I've learned that I should never trust Player 4 to catch me when doing a trust fall.*

Player 4: *I've learned that Player 3 doesn't give a long enough warning that they're about to do a trust fall.*

In the above examples, Players 1 and 2 have said things based on story elements from the show. Players 3 and 4 are commenting on something that happened during the show from the perspective of them doing the performance.

How Does the Game End?

Once all players have had their turn.

Pro Tips:

Pro Tip #1: Make a few mental notes of things that happen throughout the show that may be fun to call back to for this sequence.

Pro Tip #2: This segment is like giving 'the moral of the story' for your show. It can be an opportunity to squeeze one more laugh out of something funny or noteworthy that happened earlier.

59: CORRECTIONS

Emcee Intro Script: Just before we get into all of the fun and mayhem of our improv games today, there are a few corrections that we should note from our previous show.

Challenge Style: Chain game

Players: 1+

Ask the Audience For: Not needed for this game.

How to Play the Game:

#1: Players take turns to step forward and say their example of something that needs correcting from the previous show.

#2: The corrections don't actually need to relate to anything that happened in your previous show.

The idea of the game is to say corrections in an honest and conciliatory way as if you made factual errors in the previous show, and that you owe it to the public to correct the misinformation. You will paint a picture of the previous show, so that they can only imagine what fun and salacious scenes they missed last time.

They probably won't take the ideas seriously, but these corrections are a nice way to set the tone for the show you're about to do.

For example:

Player 1: *We need to correct the information said during our last show, as we have since been informed that the British Royal Family are not in fact lizard people... even if rumours do persist to the contrary. Your majesty, we apologise for this mix up.*

Player 2: *And I personally was wrong to imply that applying neat lemon juice followed by a sprinkle of salt will heal most cuts and bruises. I was not feeling myself that day, and my actions to claim this were malicious and out of character for me. I hope you'll respect my privacy during this difficult time.*

Player 3: *I too would like to apologise on behalf of Gus, who couldn't be in the show tonight. For obvious reasons... He's still finishing up his sentence, but we're assured that if his appeal goes through, he'll be back for next week's show.*

As you'll see from the above examples, they give enough information to make it sound like some controversial things were said and done in the previous show, but they are lacking enough details so that the audience will be left wondering exactly what happened.

You'll also note that the players gave corrections that were a mix of general mistakes made by the cast, apologising for an individual's mistake and apologising on behalf of someone else.

How Does the Game End?

The game ends once all the performers have said their corrections.

Pro Tips:

Pro Tip #1: The corrections don't always have to be something negative. You are free to go in the opposite direction. For example, you could correct that someone was actually a six time champion instead of the previously stated three time champion. I'd still be inclined to make some funny observation after something like this though, as a more positive correction may feel a little flat. But certainly, having a more cheery approach will mean that not all the corrections end up feeling samey.

Pro Tip #2: I would generally advise against performers doing callbacks or references to actual previous shows. Unless you have the exact same audience, you'll have instantly alienated anyone new if they need knowledge of the previous show to understand your reference.

Of course, if you do regular shows and know you have a regular audience, you could get away with referring to a previous show. I'd still say it's better to make every show as self-contained as possible.

60: SPELLING BEE

Emcee Intro Script: We're now going to have a Spelling Bee! Our performers will be challenged to spell words to show that they have a true mastery over both the written and spoken language.

Challenge Style: Chain game

Players: 2+

Ask the Audience For: Suggestions of words they would like the performers to spell

How to Play the Game:

#1: Either the Emcee, or another player should take on the role of the person hosting the spelling bee. They can either call up one other player who will be tasked with spelling the next word, or they can call up two players at a time like it's a competition between the two of them.

#2: The Emcee should ask the audience for a random word for the player to spell. The Emcee should then repeat it back to the player who has to spell it. The request can be as open as *'please suggest a random word'*, or the Emcee can be more specific in their request. They could ask for a particular type of word like an adjective or noun, or they could ask for a foreign word or a made-up word.

#3: Unlike an actual spelling bee, the performer tasked with spelling has a little more grace for dialogue rather than just spelling the word. They could give a couple of sentences to show how confident or unconfident they are with the word. They could also tell a short story for why they know how to spell the word. This shouldn't go on too long and the Emcee can push them to spell the word if they seem like they are stalling.

#4: The performer who is spelling the word can either genuinely attempt to spell the word or can purposely get it right or wrong based on what persona and character they are portraying for the game.

My suspicion is that if a player purposely misspells a word that the audience would expect them to know, this won't sit well with the audience. Doing this may take them out of the game slightly. I don't expect that simply spelling an easy word wrong will be enough to make the game entertaining.

#5: Once the player has spelt their word, the Emcee can announce if they have got it right or wrong and congratulate or commiserate them as appropriate.

If there are multiple players taking part to spell words, the Emcee could continue onwards with the competition as a tournament or a best of three or five to win.

How Does the Game End?

Once all the players who will be spelling words have had their turns.

Pro Tips:

Pro Tip #1: In this game you can have fun with a biased judge/referee/Emcee. They could purposely always give hard words for one player whilst giving easy words for another. If handled correctly, you may even find that the audience collude in this and take sides to purposely favour one performer with easier or harder words.

Pro Tip #2: One thing for the Emcee/judge to keep in mind is that they themselves may not know the correct spellings for some of the words. If a spelling isn't known, the Emcee could turn to the audience for advice on whether the player spelled the word correctly or not.

You also have the option to play it that the Emcee may be too proud to admit that they don't know a correct spelling themselves. This could lead to incorrect decisions by the Emcee, which could be done for humorous or dramatic effect.

61: SHOW AND TELL

Emcee Intro Script: OK class! It's now time for Show and Tell! In our next scene, our performers will take turns to show you what they have prepared for this week, and tell you all about it. I just really hope they didn't forget to bring something in...

Challenge Style: Turn take/monologue

Players: 1+

Ask the Audience For: The cast need to quickly go and ask to borrow objects from the audience to use for show and tell.

Setup:

The performers should go and ask audience members for something they can borrow to use for show and tell. This should be something that they have brought with them on their person.

Alternatively, the performers can dash around the venue and see if there is an object they can find to show and tell. Do be careful not to take something that would upset the venue for you to pick up and use.

If you are performing this game virtually, you could dash into another room from where you are performing and pick up an interesting object from your house *(or wherever it is you are performing from)*.

How to Play the Game:

#1: The Emcee will take on the role of a primary school teacher, and should speak to the other performers like they're children.

#2: The other performers have the option to bring the essence of childlike behaviour to the roles they play but also have free rein to play it more like themselves, or like an adult.

#3: The performers should show off their objects to the audience and tell stories about it and why they are showing it for show and tell.

How Does the Game End?

Once all the players have taken their turns, the Emcee should encourage the audience to clap as if the performers are children who have done well.

Pro Tips:

Pro Tip #1: Have fun with the object you've got. If it's something that is obviously impressive, that is great. Run with it.

If it's an object that doesn't seem worthy of showing off *(chewing gum or a pen)* then make up an elaborate story for why the item is so cool.

Pro Tip #2: Always respect the objects you use if they are not your property.

SECTION 7: MULTIPLAYER SCENE GAMES

#Here's a big bundle of games that are great for three or more players. There's a whole range of challenge types that will give you and your team some variety to get your teeth into.

A simple swanversation between a goose and a Vampire Penguin

62: HERE COMES JACK

Emcee Intro Script: Here Comes Jack!!! One of our players will be taking on the role of Jack, who will join the scene after about a minute. Before this point, our other performers are going to start the scene and talk about the impending arrival of Jack.

During this time, they will describe various behaviours, traits and quirks of Jack's, which the performer playing Jack will have to demonstrate as soon as they enter the scene.

Challenge Style: Scene based

Players: 3 Minimum

Ask the Audience For: Where the scene is taking place. Like some kind of reason for the characters to know each other or an event or job.

How to Play the Game:

#1: Two players start the scene and establish the scenario, event or location they are at.

#2: After ten to twenty seconds, one of them should note or question the arrival of another character called Jack/Jacky/Jaqueline, who they expect to also be at the same location as they are.

#3: Getting into conversation about Jack, the two characters in the scene should start commenting on observations they have about Jack. These observations should be about Jack's personality, physicality or behaviours. The player who will be playing the role of Jack should listen carefully to all these observations, as these are endowments that Jack will need to incorporate into their performance when they enter the scene.

For example:

Player 1: *Have you ever noticed that when someone laughs Jack gets really scared and curls up into a ball like a hamster?*

Player 2: *I have noticed that. So odd. But not as odd as the way Jack always shakes people's hands for uncomfortably long periods whilst making eye contact.*

Player 1: *Yeah, I hate that. I just hope he's past his habit of stealing food from the buffet and hiding it in his shorts for later.*

#4: After around one minute, or once the two performers in the scene have given plenty of endowments for Jack, one of the two should say the line *'Here comes Jack'*.

#5: At this point, the player playing Jack should enter the scene and start to interact with the other two players. The aim for Jack is to demonstrate as many of the behaviours, characteristics and quirks that the other players said about Jack as possible.

So based on the examples I gave, Jack may enter the scene and start shaking one of the other player's hands for a long while whilst making eye contact. They can still continue to talk and say anything they like relating to the scenario, but this would be one way to show that Jack is the character that the others were describing.

Jack then may continue to mime taking a sandwich out of their shirt to eat and offer a bite to another player. The other player may then laugh, and this will cause Jack to curl up in a ball.

#6: Make sure you remember to keep the scene going, and all three characters continue to keep moving the story forward. After Jack enters it shouldn't just be Jack showing off all their tricks like a dog. The idea is that the quirks will come through as the scene continues, and not just be about Jack doing their quirks.

How Does the Game End?

The game should be ended by the Emcee once all the quirks of the person playing Jack have been explored.

Pro Tips:

Pro Tip #1: If you're a player giving the endowments to Jack, make sure these are fun, but not too complicated or inappropriate for the person playing Jack to be able to do. If Jack can't or won't do the endowment, you'll just let down the audience by not fulfilling their expectation that Jack will do what the other players said.

Pro Tip #2: A big part of the fun of this game is that the person playing Jack is effectively a dancing monkey for the other players.

The other players can make Jack do things that the performer playing Jack may not want to or look silly for doing. With this in mind, the audience will be looking to the reactions of the player performing as Jack to gauge how they feel about having to do the things they are endowed to do.

There is therefore more of a duality of Jack also being seen as the player as well.

If Jack is endowed as *'liking to sing Madonna's song Like a Virgin whilst doing a tap dance every time someone coughs'* the other players can purposely keep coughing during the scene to force Jack to have to repeat this sequence.

This gives all the player's a chance to show a moment of them reacting as themselves as well as the character they are playing in the scene.

Even if the player has fun doing it, a brief moment where Jack shows resentment for having to keep doing this, and the delight of the other players for making Jack repeat this will go down well with the audience.

63: MISS CHARACTERISATION

Emcee Intro Script: Our next game is called Miss Characterisation. Two players will await the arrival of a third, who for the sake of this game we'll refer to as Miss Characterisation. Before Miss Characterisation arrives, the others will spread some rumours and gossip about her. After a while, Miss Characterisation, who has just been mischaracterised will arrive, and we'll see how they all react to one another with the rumours in the air.

Challenge Style: Scene based

Players: 3+

Ask the Audience For: A way in which a group of people may know each other.

Note: This game is almost like a reverse game of Here Comes Jack. It works on the same principal of characters discussing and saying characteristics and behaviours of another character before they arrive, but unlike Here Comes Jack, the characteristics they are assigning to Miss Characterisation aren't true. And the characters saying these things are either lying, misinformed or spreading rumours.

How to Play the Game:

#1: Two characters start a scene and establish the scenario.

#2: During the first minute of the scene, one or more characters should mention that Miss Characterisation will soon arrive. The characters start spreading rumours on things they have heard about Miss Characterisation who isn't present. These rumours may relate to things Miss Characterisation is supposed to have done, ways she carries on or behaves, or about her values or beliefs.

Here are some examples:

Player 1: *Be careful around Miss Characterisation. I don't mean to spread rumours, but I heard that she never washes her hands after going to the bathroom.*

Player 2: *Disgusting. But I thought you were going to say that if you turn your back, she may start sniffing your hair. I've seen her do it.*

Player 1: *I think she only does that so she has an excuse if you catch her stealing your wallet out your back pocket. It's best never to turn your back on Miss Characterisation.*

Things like this are examples of lies or rumours about Miss Characterisation, which Miss Characterisation then wouldn't do when she enters the scene. But things like this will give the other players something to act wary of.

#3: After about a minute, Miss Characterisation should enter the scene. When she does, the other characters should shush themselves with the awareness that they don't wish to be caught gossiping.

#4: The scene will now continue, but the other characters who were gossiping should react badly to the presence of Miss Characterisation.

Using the examples given, the other players are likely to refuse shaking Miss Characterisation's hand and are likely to avoid turning their backs on her. The audience will understand why they are responding this way, but the performer playing Miss Characterisation will have to act as if they are unaware of why they are being treated the way they are.

#5: The longer the scene goes on, the more obvious it should be that the other players are responding badly to Miss Characterisation.

After a while, Miss Characterisation should start to get suspicious about why she is being responded to in the way that she is. It may be that she too has heard the rumours and then tries to reassure the others it is just gossip and she is not sure how they started.

Another option could be that she accuses the other characters of spreading these rumours.

A third option is that it could turn out that some or all of the rumours are true. I would say to use this option sparingly, as the idea of the game is that these are rumours that aren't true.

How Does the Game End?

The game ends when the Emcee feels the scene has played out.

Pro Tips:

Pro Tip #1: Miss Characterisation should listen carefully to the rumours that the other players are establishing. Although the idea is that the rumours will not prove to be true, she could purposely do things that will make the other characters believe that they are.

For example, if the rumour was that Miss Characterisation doesn't wash her hands, she should absolutely keep going to shake hands or make contact with her hands to the other players.

Pro Tip #2: An optional way to play the game is that just Player 1 is spreading the rumours, and Player 2 just believes them. This can be fun as it then isn't everyone being unfair to spread rumours about Miss Characterisation. Instead, it is just one awful person who is behind all of the rumours.

Pro Tip #3: Rumours can also be that the character did something positive that they then can't live up to.

Clowning around is fun with friends

64: DIRECTORS COMMENTARY

Emcee Intro Script: In this next game, there will be two or three performers creating a scene, but as they create it, two more performers will provide Directors Commentary. As the scene goes on, our Directors will talk about how they directed the scene, the choices they made when writing it, and tell enjoyable anecdotes about the creative process.

Challenge Style: Scene based

Players: 4+

Ask the Audience For: The name of a made-up movie that doesn't already exist.

Setup: Two or more players will move about on the stage to create the scene. Another two players will play the Director/Writer, and will ideally sit together somewhere in the audience, or alternatively, stand to one side of the stage so they can observe the scene in progress.

How to Play the Game:

#1: The players in the scene will create the story, whilst the Commentators will give insight and anecdotes as to how the scene was created.

#2: All players involved should take care to really listen to one another. The Commentators will need to react to what the performers in the scene are doing. Equally to this, the performers in the scene will need to listen to what the Commentators are saying.

The reason for this is because although no one involved in the game will know exactly how the scene will progress storyline wise, from the Commentator's perspective, they are watching and commentating on a scene that has already been filmed from a movie that has already been completed and released.

As such, the Commentators may give clues to what should happen next. If one were to comment that the upcoming action sequence took four days to choreograph, the players in the scene will need to do something to reflect this. Likewise, if the Commentators mention how the scene contains their favourite twist from the movie, that is a cue for the players in the scene to include some kind of twist.

#3: To further clarify the previous point, it isn't that the Commentators get to make all the decisions about what happens in the scene. That will still be mostly up to the performers creating the scene on stage. But there is the sense that the players on the stage and the players providing the commentary need to work together to get best results out of the game's potential.

How Does the Game End?

The Emcee can end it, or it could be one of the Commentators that acknowledges that they have reached the end of the scene.

Pro Tips:

Pro Tip #1: The Commentators have the fun position of being able to say about things that will happen in the scene before they happen. This can be fun to play with as the audience will understand that the Commentators have a degree of power to make the performers in the scene have to go through with anything the Commentators establish will happen in the scene.

Pro Tip #2: The Commentators and the performers in the scene need to be really careful not to overlap dialogue too much. The performers on stage will need to leave a little breathing room between lines, and fill this with physical action so there are chances for the Commentators to talk.

The Commentators can also hold a pause on what they are saying to make sure they hear important lines from the film.

65: SLEEPER AGENT

Emcee Intro Script: In our next game, we'll meet a group of characters where they aren't aware that one of them is actually a Sleeper Agent working for an evil government. In fact, the Sleeper Agent doesn't even realise it themselves, as they were brainwashed. They will only spring into action if their activation keyword is said by another character.

Challenge Style: Scene based

Players: 2+

Ask the Audience For: Firstly, ask the audience what the Sleeper Agent's mission is. This could be something unusual.

Secondly you need to ask the audience for what their activation and deactivation words are. It could be one word, or two separate words.

How to Play the Game:

#1: The performers should start the scene with the goal of establishing the location and any activities that they may be taking part in. They should also aim to lay some groundwork for whatever the Sleeper Agent's mission may be.

For example, if the Sleeper Agent is on a mission to steal some documents or assassinate someone, the characters should casually mention things that will establish that the mission will be possible in this location.

#2: At some point in the scene, one of the characters who isn't the Sleeper Agent should say the activation word.

#3: As soon as the activation word is said, the Sleeper Agent should activate into mission mode. This should be visual and clear when it happens. Ways to achieve this may be that they stand up straighter, their speech gets interrupted, their accent changes, there is a personality shift, and they become much more focussed on their mission.

It could even be that their mission mode is like them going into a trance...or coming out of one. However you wish to play it, as soon as they are activated, they should start to do things towards completing their mission.

#4: It should be clear that the Sleeper Agent is no longer engaging with the same activities as the other characters, and are instead doing their mission.

#5: For the other characters, I would suggest that they not realise that the Sleeper Agent character is behaving unusually, or at least not at first. The longer the scene goes on, the more the other characters may become aware that something odd is happening.

#6: I would avoid the Sleeper Agent completing their mission too quickly, if at all. The best way to do this is for the other characters to find reasons to say the deactivation word to interrupt whatever the Sleeper Agent is trying to achieve.

How Does the Game End?

If the other players realise who the Sleeper Agent really is, we should see their reaction, and then the Emcee should end it. If they don't realise, the Emcee should just look for a suitable ending point.

Pro Tips:

Pro Tip #1: The non Sleeper Agent characters need to find natural reasons to say the activation and deactivation words. They should be said within regular dialogue, in a way so that it is believable that they would say the words without knowing that they hold any special meaning.

66: IMAGINARY FRIEND

Emcee Intro Script: It's time to play with our Imaginary Friend! Something many of us can relate to from our childhoods, and possibly still today. One of the performers will be playing the imaginary friend of another performer. The other characters in the scene won't be able to see, hear or interact with the Imaginary Friend character.

Challenge Style: Scene based

Players: 3+

Ask the Audience For: A location or profession

How to Play the Game:

#1: The performers create a scene, but one actor is playing the role of an Imaginary Friend to another character. Let's say the character with the imaginary friend is called Jill.

#2: None of the other performers should acknowledge the existence of the Imaginary Friend except Jill, as they wouldn't be able to see or hear them. With this in mind, the performer playing the Imaginary Friend shouldn't physically interact with any of the other actors.

#3: The Imaginary Friend can say things to Jill to influence Jill's behaviour or decision making. It could be that the Imaginary Friend is a bad influence on Jill.

The choice is yours for how you wish to develop the nature of the relationship between the Imaginary Friend and Jill. It may be that they are genuine best friends, or it may be that the Imaginary Friend is someone Jill has been trying to ignore her whole life.

How Does the Game End?

The game ends when the Emcee feels the game has reached a high point.

Pro Tips:

Pro Tip #1: Even though the characters who can't see the Imaginary Friend shouldn't say anything that acknowledges the existence of the imaginary character, you can play with this slightly.

If the Imaginary Friend says something, another character who can't hear them could say the same thing as if it is a coincidence. Or they say something that purposely contradicts the will of the Imaginary Friend. You just have to be careful not to break the rule and respond to the Imaginary Friend if you can't hear them.

Pro Tip #2: You have the option for it to be known or discovered during the scene that Jill has an imaginary friend. How would others respond to this revelation? Or maybe they've always known and think Jill is crazy or humour her for having an Imaginary Friend.

Variation:

You could play this game as a four hander or more, and have multiple characters have Imaginary Friends. You should decide in advance of playing the game if the imaginary friends can see each other or not.

As the idea of an imaginary friend is that they are imaginary to the individual who sees them, it probably should be that they can't see or interact with each other.

67: HALLUCINATIONS

Emcee Intro Script: Our next game is called Hallucinations. In the scene, one of our performers will experience delusions, hallucinations and paranoia. They will react to things that are not really there, and we'll see how they and the other characters deal with this situation.

Challenge Style: Scene based

Players: 2+

Note: This game could easily become about making light of mental health concerns, and a character just being seen as crazy by the others. This isn't the intent of the game, and how it is played is up to the individuals to agree upon the expected tone in rehearsals.

Ask the Audience For: An activity or place of work.

They could also nominate which player is the one seeing things that aren't really there.

How to Play the Game:

#1: The characters should establish the scene and characters.

#2: As the scene progresses, we should increasingly see one character reference and react to things that the other characters cannot see. The other characters may or may not instantly understand that the character hallucinating is seeing things. They should probably pick up on this quite quickly.

#3: There could be several explanations for why the character is having hallucinations. This could be that there is a gas leak, or they have eaten something bad, taken the wrong medicine, or they hit their head. Maybe they were abducted by aliens or are psychic. Whatever the reason is, it could be something you explore in the scene or not.

#4: The fun of the scene will come in seeing the character having the hallucinations and reacting to them, and the other characters trying to figure out what Is going on.

How Does the Game End?

At the Emcee's discretion.

Pro Tips:

Pro Tip #1: The character having the hallucinations should be very specific in what their hallucinations are. They will have to decide how they react to them, and communicate what the hallucinations are to both the audience and the other players.

If they are continuously vague with what they are reacting to, it'll be harder for everyone else to build a picture of what the hallucinations are in their mind's eye.

For example, if the player is hallucinating that there is a fire, they could shout *'fire!'* and then try to stamp it out. They could even encourage another player to stamp it out with them, but the other player would have to make it clear that they don't believe they are stamping out anything.

68: VOICE OF GOD

Emcee Intro Script: Our next game is Voice of God! All our performers will come together in a big huddle and deliver some words of wisdom.

But each player can only say one word at a time. There is no set order that the players have to speak in. As long as no player says two words in a row themselves, they can speak in any order.

Challenge Style: Storytelling/Group monologue

Players: 3+ (Ideally 5+)

Ask the Audience For: A subject that they need advice for.

How to Play the Game:

#1: The players stand in a big huddle. Ideally there shouldn't be an obvious order to the formation. Players can be at differing height levels such as standing, sitting or crouching. The less order there is to the formation the better.

#2: When the game begins, the players take turns to contribute one word at a time to create a group monologue. A player can only say one single word at a time, and then that player cannot speak again until after someone else has spoken.

#3: The speech created by the group should sound like a monologue as if only one character is speaking. In this sense the players shouldn't reply to each other as if it were back and forth dialogue. It should have the characteristics of a single speech. For example:

Player 1: *Remember*

Player 2: *To*

Player 3: *Be*

Player 2: *Nice*

Player 3: *To*

Player 1: *Your*

Player 5: *Best*

Player 2: *Friend*

You'll notice from this example that there was no set order to when any individual player contributed a word to the speech. One player can contribute multiple words more frequently than others as long as they only contribute one word at a time.

How Does the Game End?

Ideally the players should be able to draw this game to a close themselves without the need of the Emcee to end it for them. The advice given by the players could last from thirty seconds to a minute, or more if it has a good flow.

If the players are not building to a natural conclusion, the Emcee could cut them off, but ideally, you'll want the speech to last a minimum of a few sentences, so it feels the topic has been properly covered.

Pro Tips:

Pro Tip #1: Listen to each other! This is a group storytelling game. Make sure you really take in what has been established, and build upon the ideas.

Pro Tip #2: Try not to talk over other players. The biggest challenge of this game is that it is probable that two or more players may go to say a word at the same time. Really listen to each other and endeavour to speak when the opportunity feels right. Be very prepared to pull back on a word if you speak at the same time as another player.

Pro Tip #3: Don't feel the need to rush, but don't allow it to go so slow that it becomes dull. One way to avoid talking over each other is to not rush into saying words too fast. Other players will hear if you take a breath in ready to say something and this gentle sound of you inhaling is a good warning system for other players that you intend to say the next word. This said, be aware that this can make things feel a bit slow and if the audience pick up on this tactic it will remove the sense of challenge for them.

69: FANATICAL

Emcee Intro Script: Our next game is called Fanatical. The performers are going to get on with an everyday task or problem, but the way they handle it is going to be inspired by their being huge fans of something you suggest.

Challenge Style: Scene based

Players: 2+

Ask the Audience For: Firstly, ask for an everyday task that the characters will attempt to achieve.

Secondly, ask for something all the characters will be fans of. This could be something like a movie or book, or sport or activity. Whatever it is, it shouldn't be too closely linked to what the task is that the characters are trying to achieve.

For example, if the task is that they're sailing a boat, the thing that they are fans of shouldn't be something like fishing. You'll want the task and the thing they're fans of to be quite distinct from one another.

How to Play the Game:

#1: The characters should establish what it is they are trying to achieve and also how they know each other.

#2: As they attempt to do whatever it is they are trying to achieve, they should do it in ways that are inspired by what they are fanatical about.

So, if they are trying to sail a boat, and are huge Harry Potter fans, they may attempt to make things work with magic spells. If they are trying to cook a chicken, and they are big football fans, they might talk about achieving their *'goal'* and pass the chicken back and forth like they are playing keepy uppy.

How Does the Game End?

By the Emcee, once the performers resolve the task.

Pro Tips:

Pro Tip #1: Don't forget that the characters are trying to achieve something within the scene. It isn't just about slotting in references to the thing that the characters are fans of. Make sure you continue to drive the scene forwards.

It can be easy to fall into the trap of just making references to the thing that you are fans of and lose sight of what the scene is actually meant to be about.

Pro Tip #2: Keep the scene based within reality. Just because the characters are fans of Harry Potter doesn't mean that they can suddenly perform magic.

I know I've read the safety instructions for the last game,

but has Matt?

70: CHOOSE YOUR OWN ADVENTURE

Emcee Intro Script: It's usual in improv for us to create scenes and stories based on audience suggestions, but for our next challenge, we're going to give the audience even more control over the story than usual. This is a Choose Your Own Adventure scene. As the scene progresses, I *(the Emcee)* will periodically call out *'freeze'* and present you with multiple choices for what the characters should do next.

Challenge Style: Scene based/Long form

Note: This game format could be lengthened into a full-length long form improvised play. I won't discuss that fully in this book, and will expand on this in a future Extreme Improv book looking at long form formats. As the game is presented here, the game could be played as a single scene, or a collection of shorter scenes as a 'mini long form'.

If you wish to explore it as a long form format now, you can just extend the length of scenes, have more performers involved, and have more scenes to tell a longer story. My best advice would be to experiment with it in rehearsals and find what works for you.

Players: 3+

Ask the Audience For: Something the characters are trying to achieve

How to Play the Game:

#1 Based on the initial audience suggestion, the performers start a scene.

#2: Periodically, the Emcee should call out *'freeze'* and the performers in the scene should physically freeze and pause the scene.

The Emcee should then ask the audience to pick between two options of what the characters should do next in the scene. Once the audience have chosen the option, it is then up to the performers to follow through and develop the scene based on the audience's choice.

#3: The timing of when the Emcee should call out freeze can be handled in a couple of ways.

A: Emcee led: This would be when the Emcee calls out freeze and gives the audience two random options based on what the Emcee would like the characters/performers to do next. One or both of the options given may have nothing to do with what the characters are currently doing in the scene.

B: Performer led: This is when the performers create options within the story themselves. It may be that one character wants to go left into the forest, and the other character wants to go right, into the town. The performers/characters could just bash out the decision and decide which way go to within the scene themselves, but if the Emcee sees that the characters are creating a branched path of options, it would be a good opportunity to call out freeze.
And for clarity, it should always be the Emcee that calls freeze and not the performers in the scene themselves.

#4: Depending on how many players take part in the scene, you could have one or two consistent characters, and then any additional performers could enter and exit the scenes as various roles who the 'main characters' meet along the way.

How Does the Game End?

This game ends once the characters have accomplished whatever it is they are trying to achieve. As the game is based on the 'choose your own adventure' book format, I would suggest that there are a few short scenes which feature half a dozen to a dozen opportunities for the Emcee to ask the audience to choose what the characters do next.

Pro Tips:

Pro Tip #1: Performers in the scene should make sure they fulfil the requests of the audience once they've chosen an option. If they choose the characters to go into the forest, but the actors decide *'nah, let's leave the forest and go back to the town instead'* it'll feel like the performers went against the audience's choice and defeat the purpose of the game.

Pro Tip #2: The performers in the scene should look for opportunities to create branching options for the Emcee to get the audience to pick between. This can be about decisions of which way to go, whether to handle a situation calmly or with anger, or something as simple as what they should have to eat. Things like this work well in this game.

Pro Tip #3: The Emcee can use freezing the characters as a way to steer the story in a more helpful direction if the Emcee judges that the story is not progressing.

For the most part, I would suggest that the Emcee let the performers drive the story forward and only intervene if the story gets stuck going nowhere or in a controversial direction. As the Emcee gets to facilitate the direction of the story, they can present the audience with options to choose between. This can help move the scene on from being stuck.

Including a unicorn in your adventure scene would be on point

71: OLD JOB NEW JOB

Emcee Intro Script: The next challenge is called Old Job, New Job. Two players will start a scene where they will establish that they need the assistance of the soon to arrive Player 3. When Player 3 arrives, they will handle the situation in the style of whatever their old job was.

Challenge Style: Scene based

Players: 3

Ask the Audience For: What the old and new job of Player 3 should be.

How to Play the Game:

#1: The two players who start the scene should establish the scenario and highlight that they'll need someone who can do whatever the audience suggested the 'new job' was. This could be something like a handyman, or a doctor or a computer technician.

#2: After thirty seconds to a minute, Player 3 should come in to address what the other characters need them for.

#3: The way Player 3 should approach doing the new job should be in the same manner how they would have approached doing whatever their old job was. For example:

If the characters need a computer technician, but the technician's old job was that they were a hunter, they may sneak up on the computer and switch it off by surprise. They may also put some cheese down to trap the computer mouse, and could catch the computer in an 'inter...net'

How Does the Game End?

When Player 3 has finished helping the others with what they needed achieving.

Pro Tips:

Pro Tip #1: The way the old job/new job character should approach things is to make it clear that they are doing whatever their new job is, but with language and actions that would have been more befitting of their old job.

Pro Tip #2: The characters who need the help of Player 3 who has the old/new job can choose how they react to Player 3's unconventional approach. Maybe they just trust them because *'they're the expert'* or maybe they find the whole affair quite bizarre.

Old Job: Burglar

New Job: Night watchman

72: AM DRAM

Emcee Intro Script: We are now going to play Am Dram! Our performers will create a scene in a purposely amateur dramatics style.

Challenge Style: Scene based

Players: 2+

Ask the Audience For: A well-known real-world event. This can either be something from history, or it can be something from the recent news.

How to Play the Game:

#1: The players should start the scene and establish the scenario.

#2: This game is all about purposely acting in an amateur style. Purposely being over the top, talking over one another, forgetting lines, mumbling, facing the back of the stage, being monotone and approaching the subject matter with the wrong tone are all ways to achieve this.

How Does the Game End?

When the Emcee decides they have explored the theme for the scene.

Pro Tips:

Pro Tip #1: The idea is that you'll want the audience to recognise what you're doing as 'bad acting'. The aim is that both you and the audience are in on the joke.

To purposely act bad, you'll actually need to be pretty good. To purposely go wrong, you'll need to know what are the right things to do, and then intentionally not do them.

Even if you do demonstrably bad acting, you should still be careful to make sure the audience can always see and hear you, and follow the story.

73: GAG REFLEX

Emcee Intro Script: Our next game is called Gag Reflex. Two players will begin a scene as if they are having a private conversation. A third player will enter and not be part of the conversation but will be eavesdropping their conversation and periodically interject and say puns based on whatever they're talking about.

Challenge Style: Scene based

Players: 3

Ask the Audience For: Where the characters are meeting.

How to Play the Game:

#1: The two characters who already know each other should begin a conversation with the third lingering in the background. Maybe they are familiar with one another, but this third character shouldn't actively be part of the conversation.

#2: The Eavesdropping Character should periodically make quips and puns on whatever the other characters are talking about. They should look for natural pauses in the conversation for these interjections. This can be at the end of sentences, where there are small gaps that they can speak in. For example:

Player 1: *My brother-in-law is a police officer. Did you know that?*

Player 2: *Is that the one with a beard?*

Eavesdropping Character: *The one with the fuzz...*

Player 1: *Yes, he did have a beard, but he's shaved it now.*

Player 2: *I didn't know he was a cop. I've never seen him in uniform.*

Player 1: *He works mostly undercover.*

Eavesdropping Character: *Under the covers. Like pigs in blankets.*

Player 1: *Do you mind? We're not talking to you.*

#3: The other players should intentionally give space within the conversation for the Eavesdropping Character to quip in, but these should only be fleeting. If they don't interject with a pun, the others should just move on and continue the conversation.

#4: The two characters having the conversation may or may not overhear the quips and react to them, but their aim should be to continue to have a private conversation.

If they do become aware of the person making these puns, you can choose how they react to this. Maybe they are mildly amused, or think the person is being rude. Whatever the case, I'd avoid bringing them into the conversation too much as it'll change the format of the game.

How Does the Game End?

At the Emcee's discretion.

Pro Tips:

Pro Tip #1: The Eavesdropping Character should have a purpose for being at the location as well. Maybe they're waiting for someone, or on a phone call, or having a drink alone. At some point the other characters may address them and ask why they are interjecting, so be prepared with an answer. It shouldn't be that they are only there to watch and listen in to the others.

74: ALL ABOUT ME

Emcee Intro Script: This next game is All About Me….sorry I mean it is called All About Me. There will be three or four performers in the scene, but no matter what is going on with anyone else, there will be that one person who tries to make everything about themselves.

Challenge Style: Scene based

Players: 3+

Ask the Audience For: A reason why a group of people may know each other or something that a group of people may be working on.

One player should also be assigned as the Self-Centred Character. As an option, the audience could pick one of the performers to play this role.

How to Play the Game:

#1: The performers should start a normal scene where they establish who the characters are and what it is they are trying to achieve.

#2: Continuously throughout the scene, the Self-Centred Character should look for opportunities to make whatever is being said, or whatever is going on, about themselves.

The ways you find to do this are up to you. It may be that anything that is going on reminds them of something that happened to them, and they have to share a story or example.

It could be that they always want to be the person to do something instead of someone else. They may also place more importance on their reactions or feelings over others.

#3: You can decide how much the other characters choose to acknowledge the Self-Centred Character's behaviour or not. Maybe they are used to it, or maybe they get frustrated at it.

If it's the latter, it's even more likely that the Self-Centred Character will make the way others are reacting to them about themselves.

How Does the Game End?

The Emcee should end the scene.

Pro Tips:

Pro Tip #1: The Self-Centred Character could be oblivious to their selfishness, and find opportunities to project their behaviour onto others.

For example:

Player 1: *I think I'm having chest pains.*

Self-Centred Character: *Oh my goodness, I was just saying yesterday that I always am having chest pains.*

Player 1: *I think I'm having a heart attack.*

Self-Centred Character: *It's not always about you! I was just saying that I was having pain yesterday. But then I had a big glass of milk...*

Player 1: *I think I'm dying...*

Self-Centred Character: *It's always me me me me with you. Anyway, stand back everyone and watch me save a life. Make sure you're filming.*

75: AN APOLOGY ABOUT LAST NIGHT

Emcee Intro Script: This game is called An Apology About Last Night, and in it, there is one very Hung Over Character after last night's drinking activities. This morning, the Hung Over Character cannot remember anything they did the night before. But, whatever it is that they did, they managed to upset all the other characters. I think it's time they faced the music.

Challenge Style: Scene based

Players: 3+

Ask the Audience For: A suggestion of where the characters were last night.

How to Play the Game:

#1: The game should start with two characters. Player 1 is the Hung Over Character. In the opening of the game, you'll need to establish that they are just meeting Player 2 the next morning. Also the Hung Over Character has no idea as to what happened the night before.

#2: Player 2 should give some details of what happened the night before, but be purposely vague.

Player 2 should start to remind the Hung Over Character of what they did. As the Hung Over Character is reminded of what they did the night before, the Hung Over Character should start to remember.

#3: As the Hung Over Character is reminded of what they did, it will be the responsibility of both players to add details to what happened. For example:

Player 2: *Do you not remember what you did with the pen last night?*

Hung Over Character: *Oh my god, I drew a moustache on the painting of your nan, didn't I?*

Player 2: *That wasn't a painting.*

Hung Over Character: *Oh no! You mean I draw the moustache on your actual nan's face?*

As seen in the example, both characters will build up the picture of what happened the night before. These can be simple, or they can get quite elaborate.

#4: Once what happened the night before has been revealed, the Hung Over Character should apologise. It's up to the performers whether Player 2 accept the apology or not. Either way, after this, Player 2 character should reveal that what the Hung Over Character did to them was nothing compared to what they did to Player 3.

#5: At this point Player 3 should enter the scene. They will be even more annoyed at the Hung Over Character than Player 2, and the process will repeat.

#6: Continue this rhythm of each non hung over player introducing the next until all players have confronted the Hung Over Character.

How Does the Game End?

The game ends once all players have confronted the Hung Over Character.

Pro Tips:

Pro Tip #1: Make sure you listen to each and every player and what their experiences were with the Hung Over Character. If you can, you may be able to weave the stories of each character together. This can mean that by the end of the game we have a very clear picture of what the Hung Over Character had gotten up to the night before.

Pro Tip #2: As new players enter the scene, it could be that the other players leave, or it could just be that they take a backseat on the conversation. If they do stay active in the scene, they would be able to chip in with the next player's stories. I'd avoid them chipping in too much, as it should be just the Hung Over Character and one non hung over player building the story at a time.

76: THE BIRDS AND THE BEES

Emcee Intro Script: It's time for… THE talk. This next game is called The Birds and the Bees. Two of our performers will take on the roles of parents who are going to explain where babies come from to the third performer who will be playing their child. But as I'm sure many of our audience will appreciate, this isn't an easy talk for a parent to give. Many find it easier to talk about it with comparisons and metaphors instead of hitting the nail directly on the head.

Challenge Style: Scene based

Players: 3

Ask the Audience For: An unusual theme to compare making babies to.

How to Play the Game:

#1: You can begin the scene however you want, but a good starting point could either be the parents seeking the child out to give the talk to, or the child asking the unsuspecting parents. The fun thing in either scenario is that one half of the equation will feel caught off guard which will add to the awkwardness of the scene.

#2: The parent characters should attempt to explain where babies come from, but after introducing the idea, they should lean into whatever comparison or metaphor the audience suggested. For example:

If the audience suggested *making a cake*, you could compare mixing the ingredients needed to make a cake to needing to mix certain things together to make a baby. You could also talk about how long a cake takes to cook in the oven and how it can sometimes take up to nine months until it's just right. Stuff like this.

#3: Any or all of the characters could find the talk awkward, stressful and embarrassing. How you play it is up to you.

How Does the Game End?

Once the audience has achieved second hand embarrassment...or when the Emcee feels it's reached the end.

Pro Tips:

Pro Tip #1: You can have fun with how matter of fact or graphic you are in your description of things. You'll have to read the room to see how much you can push things, because some won't like things being too descriptive.

Pro Tip #2: The player acting as the child could choose to intentionally not understand all the examples given. Therefore, this may require the embarrassed parents to attempt to re-explain with even more elaborate descriptions.

77: SIDE EFFECTS

Emcee Intro Script: Imagine if you could take a magic pill and it gave you superpowers. Would be great right? But would it be worth being able to do amazing things if it also came with unwanted Side Effects? That is what this game is all about.

Challenge Style: Scene based

Players: 2+

Ask the Audience For: A superpower that the magical super pill will give you. This can be something expected like super strength, or something unusual like the ability to detect acid reflux in others.

Also ask the audience for an unusual side effect that comes when the pill wears off, or as an unwanted reaction.

How to Play the Game:

#1: Start the scene and establish the scenario. The Emcee could ask for a suggestion of where the characters are, but I'd suggest the performers in the scene develop what the scenario is based on what the superpower and the side effects may lend themselves to.

Ideally, the performers should establish problems within the story that the superpowers would be useful to resolve.

#2: Early into the scene, the character who is taking the super pill, should either take the pill as part of the scene, or reveal that they have already taken the pill. As the scene continues, we should see the usefulness of these powers.

#3: Also, as the scene develops, we should start to see how the side effects of the pill begin to affect the character. The characters will probably have to acknowledge the existence of these side effects within the dialogue to make them very clear for the audience.

The side effects should rapidly begin to affect the character's ability to use their superpowers, and it shouldn't be a given that the characters are able to solve the problems by the end of the scene.

How Does the Game End?

When the problem that the superpowers can resolve is resolved, or when the Emcee feels the scene has run its course.

Pro Tips:

Pro Tip #1: The character who gets the superpowers could be portrayed as a superhero, or they could be a regular person who has a super pill. It's up to you if you want other characters to know that the powers come from the pill or not, and it's something you can negotiate through the scene.

Blocking a scene partner's offer is like closing a door in their face

78: MR BRIGHTSIDE

Emcee Intro Script: Our next game is called Mr Brightside, and is about a character who keeps coming across unfortunate, unlucky or just downright bad situations. Because they are Mr Brightside, they are always able to see the positive and Brightside to everything.

Challenge Style: Scene based

Players: 2+

Ask the Audience For: Where Mr Brightside is today.

How to Play the Game:

#1: The scene should start with the performer playing Mr Brightside on stage. Before anyone else enters the scene, we should get a sense of how positive they are and happy things are for them no matter what.

#2: As the scene progresses, various performers should enter. They can either enter one at a time or together and demonstrate bad situations that seem to follow Mr Brightside around. Despite how bad whatever happens may be, it is the job of Mr Brightside to always find the positives and put a positive spin on every situation.

How Does the Game End?

Either the Emcee calls to end the scene, or it may be fun for something to finally be Mr Brightside's breaking point where they can no longer be positive. At this point the Emcee should end it.

Pro Tips:

Pro Tip #1: The players who enter the scene should quickly establish lots of different bad things that happen to or around Mr Brightside.

Things such as splashing him from a puddle, or running over his foot, or more serious things like him getting fired or lightning striking his house and burning it down.

You'll want lots of different things like this to challenge how much Mr Brightside can always stay happy and positive. Ideally these should build up in how negative they are.

Pro Tip #2: The performer playing Mr Brightside should find ways to show that they are affected negatively, but this should just be momentarily before reverting back to seeing the positives.

Seeing the positives can take the form of brushing things off as if they don't matter, or putting a spin on things to say why the negative thing that has just happened is actually in some way a good thing.

Pro Tip #3: It could be fun if the breaking point for Mr Brightside is something minor after everything else has been much more serious.

For example, if throughout the scene the characters have established that Mr Brightside has been fired, arrested, shot and his house exploded, it would be fun if the thing that drives him over the edge is that someone forgot to put sugar in his tea.

79: THREE'S A CROWD

Emcee Intro Script: Our next improv game is called Three's a Crowd. The scene will be set on a first date between two of our performers, but one of the performers will have brought someone unusual or unexpected accompanying them on the date.

Challenge Style: Scene based

Players: 3

Ask the Audience For: A suggestion of where the date is, and also who the Third Wheel is that is joining the two who are on the date. This could be someone one of them know, or someone more random, but I'd lean towards having someone with some connection to one of the other characters.

How to Play the Game:

#1: The scene should start with the dating characters who we'll call Mae and June meeting for the date. It should be noticed that one of Mae and June has brought someone along with them, who will need introducing.

#2: Mae and June should then attempt to have a normal date and get to know each other as they would when first going out. However, they will have the unusualness of there being a third and unexpected person also there with them.

#3: It's up to you if/how you want to explain who the Third Wheel is, and why they have been brought along.

It could be as simple as a guy saying he brought his mother along, or a girl saying she promised her best friend she could come too. It could be for emotional support, that they are an inseparable friend, or a court ordered chaperone. You can really be creative and use your imagination for the justification for why the Third Wheel is there.

#4: The person playing the Third Wheel should focus on making their presence uncomfortable for the dating couple. It doesn't have to be that they are purposely trying to sabotage the date, but their very presence should be enough to make things difficult.

How Does the Game End?

The game ends when we get to the end of the date, and we get a sense if Mae and June would be willing to go out with one another again in the future.

Pro Tips:

Pro Tip #1: Ultimately, it is the rules of the game that dictate that the Third Wheel is always present at the date. This is important to keep in mind, as I'm sure in most cases, a character who truly was being a third wheel would pick up on it and either excuse themselves or be asked to leave.

In this game, the character who is the Third Wheel should act like it is normal and expected for them to be included on the date. You could have characters acknowledge that it is weird for the Third Wheel to be there, but even if you do this, the Third Wheel should still not offer to leave.

Pro Tip #2: The date can be multiple parts and doesn't just have to be set during dinner or drinks or at one location. As long as you make the activities of the date clear, feel free to have the date include different activities. It could start at dinner and move onto bowling or the cinema.

SECTION 8: SPECIFIC GOALS

These games are about a specific goal. Something you must do or must not do in a scene. Sometimes you'll have the goal to make another player do something, and other times it'll be that you have to avoid doing something the others are trying to make you do.

If you believe in yourself, you can achieve any goal!

That's a reach...

80: PERSUASION

Emcee Intro Script: The game we're going to play now is called Persuasion and is a scene for two players. In it, Player 1 will be tasked with the objective that they have to persuade Player 2 to do something that they don't want to do. This could be something serious like getting a doctor or lawyer to break confidence, convincing a person to cheat on their wife, lie to their boss, or something more trivial like insisting that the other person let you pay the bill, or go to prison for you. Trivial stuff like that.

Here's the catch. The player being persuaded can't just say no for the sake of saying no. We want to see both players being very creative in this negotiation.

Challenge Style: Objective/Scene based

Players: 2

Ask the Audience For: A suggestion of what Player 1 will need to convince Player 2 to do.

How to Play the Game:

#1: The opening of the scene should be to establish who the characters are and perhaps what they are doing or where the scene is taking place.

#2: After this is done, it's time to get down to business. Player 1 should start working towards their goal. They could address what they want to persuade Player 2 to do directly, or could be more sly.

#3: Player 2 should find every justification for why they shouldn't be persuaded. But...they can't just say no for the sake of no. The objective of the game for both players is to find loop holes and wiggle room, and increasingly more creative reasons to persuade or not be persuaded.

How Does the Game End?

The scene will end with a crescendo where one player will admit defeat that they have succeeded or failed in their objective. If no player is budging, the Emcee can step in and ask the audience to decide if the persuader had made a convincing enough argument or not.

Pro Tips:

Pro Tip #1: The player doing the persuading should aim to build up their attempts to persuade Player 2. If they start from a position of life or death, it'll be hard to roll it back to something more mundane or trivial.

Pro Tip #2: This is an example of a game that could be played as a genuine competition, and a battle of wits for who is more creative and skilled in their debate.

However, I'd remind the players that even though you could go this route, do remember that the ultimate objective is to make the scene entertaining for the audience. As such, don't take winning or losing too seriously, and be willing to throw the fight or make concessions for the betterment of the scene, even if this means you lose ground in the argument.

Pro Tip #3: The scene will be most satisfying if the persuader is eventually able to convince the Player 2 to do the thing they don't want to do. From the audience's perspective, the challenge is on the persuader to win, not on the Player 2 to defend. But certainly, if the persuader doesn't come up with any good justifications, Player 2 should not relent.

A cheap victory won't feel satisfying for the audience if Player 2 just throws the fight in an obvious way. This said, there is of course room for one player just to give up in a *'to hell with it'* kind of way which will probably get a laugh.

81: SOLUTIONS AND EXCUSES

Emcee Intro Script: Doing things is hard. That's why I always try to avoid doing anything at all. It's much easier to get other people to do everything for you. That's what our next game, Solutions and Excuses is all about. The players will create a scene about a struggle over who will do tasks. One of them will try to come up with solutions to problems, and the other will always try to avoid taking responsibility to do things. I'm sure I've just described several relationships in the room.

Note: Unlike the game Persuasion, this game isn't about making the other player do something against their will. This game is all about both characters making excuses for not doing things, and coming up with elaborate solutions that involve them not doing tasks themselves.

Challenge Style: Scene based

Players: 2

Ask the Audience For: A type of relationship between two people. Optionally, something that needs achieving.

How to Play the Game:

#1: The opening of the scene should be to establish who the characters are and what the scenario and/or their relationship is.

#2: As the scene progresses, the players should both discover problems that need solving. This could be things like the house needs cleaning, or shelves need restocking, or something more serious like the protective shield needs activating.

#3: The players should keep finding excuses to not do the tasks themselves. They should also find solutions to the tasks that would mean the other player has to be the one to do the task instead of them.

The scene isn't just about laziness and doing nothing. Both characters should be very proactive and creative in the solutions they find to problems, but just never take the responsibility to do things themselves.

#4: The solutions and excuses should become increasingly creative and elaborate as the scene goes on. The humour is derived from it being much more effort to not do the things rather than them just doing them.

How Does the Game End?

The scene should end with a character relenting and doing something they have been avoiding doing.

Pro Tips:

Pro Tip #1: You will probably find that one player becomes more about finding solutions and the other is more about finding excuses. For example, if the characters are a parent and their child. The parent could insist the child clean their bedroom.

Even if the balance is more one sided like this, the child character should highlight other tasks the parent character could do that they likewise will then have to avoid doing.

Pro Tip #2: Don't forget that the scene still needs to be a scene and isn't just about the objective of doing or not doing things. Still move the story of the scene forward, and avoid it just becoming a constant argument.

Pro Tip #3: Even if characters are avoiding doing certain things, it doesn't mean the characters just do nothing in the scene. It could be fun to see them go to great lengths to do perhaps more difficult or costly tasks in the pursuit of not doing the thing that is being asked of them.

For example, a character could decide that rather than clean a carpet, they start talking about fitting a new one which would obviously take a lot more effort.

Variation: Rather than the game always be a battle of two characters trying to get each other to do things, you could play it as two characters who are on the same page trying to avoid a task. For example, two employees putting in a lot of effort to avoid stocking a shelf. They could agree to break each other's legs or start a protest rather than do the simple task.

82: THREE IN A BOAT

Emcee Intro Script: This next challenge is called Three in a Boat, and is a scene for three players. Unfortunately, the three characters have been involved in a horrific Titanic level boating accident. They are the only survivors to manage to get onto the ship's only lifeboat.

The characters are strangers to one another and have been drifting in the ocean for some time. They can finally see a desert island in the distance.

Unfortunately, they have also sprung a leak. If they hope to make it to the island, they will need to lessen the weight in the boat or they will sink into shark infested waters. Between them, they are going to have to decide which one of them is least useful to the future survival of the other two. Then sacrifice this person…or none of them will make it. And they have five minutes to decide who is getting off the lifeboat.

Challenge Style: Scene based

Players: 3

Ask the Audience For: Suggestions of professions or specific people who are in the lifeboat.

Setup: The three characters should all be in close proximity to one another in a clearly defined area to represent the lifeboat. One way to do this is to turn two chairs inwards facing one another and the players can only use the space between these.

How to Play the Game:

Though the scene is improvised, I would suggest that the game follows this basic formula to get the most out of it.

#1: During the opening of the scene, I would suggest the characters do a little scene setting/world building before they notice the island or that the boat is sinking. A few lines to establish who the characters are, what their personalities are like and also reference the horrific disaster that caused them to be on the lifeboat.

#2: By the end of the first minute of the scene, the characters should become aware of the island in the distance. This can be seen as their salvation, or however they would react to it.

#3: Shortly after this, the characters should also become aware of the leak in the lifeboat. This could just be coincidental, or the leak may happen as a result of something one or more of the characters do. For example, the characters may cheer and celebrate when the see the island, but then accidentally drop something that damages the lifeboat.

#4: The characters should realise that they'll never make it to the island if all three of them remain in the lifeboat as the weight of three of them will mean that they'll sink before they reach the island.

#5: Each character will have to make their case for why they should stay on the boat, and why it should be one of the others who has to go overboard. This should be done through conversation and negotiation, and trying to form alliances and teaming up with another person on the lifeboat.

As a warning, this can quickly end up as squabbling, so you'll need to find ways for it to be discussion and debate, and not just arguing.

I would recommend that characters focus on why their experience with their profession is most useful, and that they would be an asset for the best chances of survival on the island. They should highlight what skills they can contribute.

They will also have to make the case for why the others are not as useful as they are. This should lead to backstabbing and flip flopping and forming of alliances against each other.

Another tactic is to attempt to pull on each other's heart strings to justify why you should survive instead of someone else. It may be that you invent a child who depends on you, or that you argue that one of the others has lived a better life than you have, so its ok for them to sacrifice themselves so you can have your chance.

Use whatever tactics you can think of.

How Does the Game End?

The game should end between the 3-5 minute mark and should end with someone either being thrown off the boat, or sacrificing themselves.

Note: This game shouldn't ever be played with characters getting into actual pushing or shoving matches with people trying to forcibly push another character off the boat. You do have the option to play into the threat of violence, but would say unless you negotiate how you would work sequences like this in rehearsals, I would suggest not to do them.

Pro Tips:

Pro Tip #1: Remember that you're in a boat, so help visualise this for the audience. This can be achieved by how you move on the boat. Sitting and swaying or walking as if your movements are rocking the boat will help show this.

Pro Tip #2: Make sure that all players know that this is a game that can be won and lost, but not to take it so seriously that they would be upset if they are the character thrown off the boat at the end.

The characters should also absolutely try hard to form alliances and convince the others that they should live. If a character just volunteers to jump off from the beginning, it'll take away from the potential of what this game can offer.

Pro Tip #3: As a thought to contradict the previous point, you could have fun where every character ends up being the one who wants to sacrifice themselves. Each character may have nothing they want to go back to their old lives for, or they may simply want to take the glory of being the one who died to save the others.

Pro Tip #4: Remember, the waters around the boat are filled with man eating sharks. Players cannot cheat the system by saying they'll swim away and live, or that they'll attack the sharks because they know kung fu. The only way to survive is to be one of two characters who make it to the island. If anyone gets out the boat before they reach the island, they will be eaten. Also, if no one gets out the boat by the end of the game, all characters die.

83: CANNIBALS

Emcee Intro Script: Our next game is called...Cannibals. It is a game for three players, but before we begin, let me set the scene for you.

Each of our three performers will be assigned a profession or character type that they are playing. And whoever these people are, they all find themselves as the survivors of a plane crash on a desert island. Rescue has little chance of finding them, and they have no food.

Through negotiation, the players are going to have to make the hardest of choices. If two of them are going to survive, they are going to have to eat the third. How they come to this decision is up to them, but they'll have a maximum of five minutes to make this decision, or they will be deemed to have all died of starvation.

Challenge Style: Scene based

Players: 3

Ask the Audience For: A job or character type for each player such as teacher, baker, grandmother, or person with persistent hiccups.

How to Play the Game:

#1: The players have a maximum of five minutes with the objective to decide who, if anyone, they are going to sacrifice and eat to stay alive.

#2: You should still take the first minute to establish characters and the scenario. This could include trying to find help, signal for rescue, or searching for food. Only once the scenario is established should they realise that to survive, one will have to be sacrificed and eaten.

#3: The performers should not just stand there and instantly say *'well I should survive because...'* The idea of going cannibal should be something the characters think of during the course of the scene.

It can be easy to take the objective of the game *(the idea that one will end up eaten)* and not show why the characters are doing this. Even if the Emcee gives the performers this challenge, you'll still have to show the audience why the characters make this choice.

#4: Like the game Three in a Boat, this game is all about negotiation. The players should attempt to convince the others why they shouldn't be the one sacrificed and eaten, and form alliances and team up.

#5: I would say that all the performers should avoid quickly making it obvious which two are going to team up on the third. This game does have a real aspect of winning and losing, and if two quickly team up on the third for no good reason, it will take all the tension out of the game.

A huge aspect of the fun of this game is the audience seeing how well each of the performers makes their case and negotiates with the others.

#6: The performers should not resort to the characters getting physically violent to attack the others.

I would say that it is useful in the game for there to be a sense of physical menace, but the characters shouldn't physically start fighting unless you have worked out your own team's policies on using stage combat in improv.

The furthest you should take it would be a character looking ready to pounce on another, and the one who is going to be pounced on showing that they are ready to defend themselves.

If you've escalated things to any sort of violence, the scene won't really have any sense of negotiation, and the Emcee should probably intervene to end it early.

#7: Use false finishes. You could have two characters grab the third as if they are about to kill or eat them, but if you do this, you'll need to instantly find a reason to back down.

In pro wrestling terms, this would be known as a *'false finish'* where the audience will think that it's about to be over, but after a momentary crescendo, one of the players will have to change their minds.

How Does the Game End?

Within the final minute of the scene, the characters should make it clear who they are planning to eat. The characters could put it to a vote between themselves, or once the time limit has run out, the Emcee could interview the performers to vote on who will be eaten.

Pro Tips:

Pro Tip #1: Be willing to flip flop and change alliances back and forth within the scene to keep the audience guessing which way the two on one vote will go.

Pro Tip #2: Try to justify why you shouldn't be eaten in any way you can. Explain why you would be most useful for survival, pull on the heart strings of the others, and explain how you have weird diseases that would make you no good as food.

Pro Tip #3: You have the option to sacrifice yourself and volunteer to be eaten. Doing this will quickly bring the game to an end, so it may be better to save the self-sacrifice until the end of the game if that is your intention.

If you think a player is offering to sacrifice themselves to the detriment of the game, one thing you can do is not accept their willingness to be the self-sacrifice. Say that they don't get to be the martyr and offer to sacrifice yourself instead because you suddenly can't stand the idea of killing one of the others.

SECTION 9: SINGING AND DANCING

Some people say life is something of a song and dance routine. Well, these games are for those who love to sing their way through the day, and dance the night away. And on that note...here's the games.

This dude is the GOAT!!!

84: BARTENDER

Emcee Intro Script: Our next game is called Bartender, and it's a singing based challenge for two performers. In the game, one of the players will take on the role of a bartender in a pub, who will hear about the problems of their patron, and then give some advice. Both the bartender and the person playing the patron will sing throughout.

Challenge Style: Singing

Players: 2

Ask the Audience For: Something that the patron character is worried or happy about or has on their mind.

Setup: I'd recommend either having a backing track or someone play music live for this game. Ideally, the performers should have microphones to make sure they can be heard over the music. This game is often performed with a physical bar or table, and to add to the scene, props such as wine/beer glasses and beer mats can be added.

How to Play the Game:

#1: The game starts with the bartender welcoming the patron into the pub and noticing that they look down in the dumps. The bartender will then offer to hear their concerns.

#2: The patron character will sing about their concerns and problems.

#3: The bartender will then sing back some advice for the patron character.

#4: You have the option for the characters to take turns singing back and forth as they work to solve more intricate problems.

How Does the Game End?

The game ends once the song has reached an end.

Pro Tips:

Pro Tip #1: Audiences enjoy when improvised songs rhyme, so endeavour to do this if you can. Practice makes perfect in regard to building up your ability to rhyme quickly.

Pro Tip #2: Hit the final syllable of your lines in the song. If you really hit that final sound clearly, it'll make it easier to find words that rhyme.

Pro Tip #3: Take your time. The faster you sing, the less thinking time you'll have to formulate rhymes.

Pro Tip #4: Songs don't have to rhyme. They're just more satisfying when they do.

85: DANCE DETECTIVE

Emcee Intro Script: Our next game is Dance Detective. One of our performers is going to take on the role of the Dance Detective and stand blindfolded in the centre of a semicircle made up of all the other performers. Once blindfolded, I will assign one of the other performers to be the Dance Leader.

The Dance Leader will start a dance which the others will have to pick up and copy, joining in one at a time. After around thirty seconds, the Dance Detective will take their blindfold off. The Detective will then get to observe the dance routine the others have created. At the minute mark, the Detective can try to identify who is the Dance Leader.

If they guess correctly, they win! If they don't, the music will continue until they can work it out and guess again.

Challenge Style: Dancing/Guessing game

Players: 5+

Ask the Audience For: The audience could pick who the Dance Detective or Dance Leader is, but it could also just be assigned by the Emcee.

How to Play the Game:

#1: The player acting as the Dance Detective will stand centre stage and wear a blindfold over their eyes.

#2: The player acting as Dance Leader will then be assigned and highlighted to the audience by the Emcee.

#3: The music should start. Then, led by the Dance Leader, all the other performers should create a semicircle around the Dance Detective.

#4: The Dance Leader will start creating a simple dance routine that will be easy enough for the others to copy.

#5: One by one, the others should start to copy the moves and join in with the other dancers.

#6: The real challenge for the other dancers is they will have to keep an eye on the Dance Leader and do what they can to copy the Leader's moves without making it obvious that they're copying or are a step behind them.

#7: Once all the performers have joined in, the Emcee can tell the Dance Detective that they can remove the blindfold. As the others continue to dance, the Dance Detective should turn around and watch the others do the dance and try to figure out who the Dance Leader is.

#8: Once the Detective has had around another thirty seconds to observe, the Emcee can ask the Detective to guess who the Dance Leader is. If they get it right, they win and that's the end of the game. If they get it wrong, they can observe for a little while longer and try again.

How Does the Game End?

The game ends once the Dance Detective has guessed who the Dance Leader is correctly.

Pro Tips:

Pro Tip #1: Don't just stand there. If you're not the Dance Leader, but are waiting to join in their dance routine, you should still be bobbing along or doing simple steps just to keep the scene looking active and fun.

Pro Tip #2: The Dance Detective can also do some simple dance moves whilst blind folded in the centre just so they keep the sense of fun going. There's no way they'll be able to copy the Dance Leader, so their moves will be very different. As such, these can be light-hearted and silly, but shouldn't pull focus from whatever the Dance Leader would be creating.

Pro Tip #3: The Dance Detective should really try to work out who the Dance Leader is, but this being said, we don't want the game to be over instantly. I would suggest the Dance Detective take on a persona of sorts in this game. They should look inquisitive, and communicate to the audience that they are puzzled by who the Dance Leader is through their facial expressions and body language.

Pro Tip #4: The Dance Detective doesn't have to stay in the centre of the semicircle and can walk up to the other performers or even walk around the back of the circle.

Do this to give the sense that you're trying to examine the dance moves to work out who the Dance Leader is. In reality, you're just buying time to keep the game going a little longer.

Pro Tip #5: The best tactic would be to step back from the dancers to try to see them all at once. This would be the easiest way to spot who is leading. I would suggest you don't do this as it will make the game too easy and then it won't be as much fun.

Pro Tip #6: Building off the last two points, if the Dance Detective does blatantly see who the leader is, they should guess correctly so the audience doesn't think the guessing game is rigged. It isn't. But as it's a performance, you could look for ways to milk the moment.

Strut your funky stuff

86: DUET

Emcee Intro Script: Our next game is called Duet and is a singing game for two performers. You'll get to pick what or who they sing about, and then they'll create a song completely made up on the spot.

Challenge Style: Singing

Players: 2

Ask the Audience For: A volunteer to have a song made up about themselves. If you get a person out the audience, you should ask their name and a couple of other details like what they do for a living, or what their favourite hobby is.

Alternatively, if you don't want to take someone out of the audience for this game, you could ask for the name of a celebrity or character to make up the song about.

You could also ask the audience for a suggestion of genre of music for the song to be. If you do this, you'll need a large selection of backing tracks available so that you have something appropriate, or you'll need a musician who is confident they can play many styles.

Setup: For this game, you should invite the audience member to stage and have them either stand centre stage or offer them a chair to sit on. The two performers should then stand either side to sing.

How to Play the Game:

#1: The two performers creating the song should take turns to sing a verse about the person/theme for the song. I would suggest in rehearsals you organise the order of who will sing. One way to do this is to decide that whoever is stood stage right as the music starts will start the song.

#2: During the song, the performers should look for opportunities to support each other's sections by harmonising or echoing each other. This will really enhance the songs and give the sense that *"it's too good to be improvised as they were singing together"*.

#3: Try to make the lyrics clearly about the person/subject matter of the song and not just generic with the person's name thrown in.

How Does the Game End?

When the song ends.

Pro Tips:

Pro Tip #1: As soon as you know the person's name, start thinking of what words may rhyme with it and store these in your memory bank to incorporate in the song.

Pro Tip #2: Likewise, as soon as you find out their profession or hobbies, you should start thinking around the topics for what ideas link to them. For example, if a person says they are a bank manager, you can quickly think of any important words or terms that would link to a bank. Words like money, cash, vault, loan etc. Once you've thought of a few of these, think of other words that will rhyme with them.

Now here comes the clever bit.

When you're creating your rhyming lyrics, just make sure you put the important word second in the rhyming couplet. For example, if the person we are singing about is Larry who runs the bank we could come up with lyrics like the following:

Your name is Larry, but I call you honey,

You I want to marry, and spend all your money

87: IRISH DRINKING SONG

Emcee Intro Script: This next game is called Irish Drinking Song! And in the game, our performers will work together to create a jolly song where they will sing one line at a time!

Challenge Style: Singing

Players: 4

Setup: You'll need either a suitable soundtrack or someone to play a tune on an instrument such as piano or guitar.

Ask the Audience For: A topic or theme for the song to be about

How to Play the Game:

#1: You can add you own tune or style to how you play it, but as this is a game made famous by television's *Whose Line is it Anyway?* I'll describe how it is played on that version. You can check out many videos to see the style and hear the kind of music you could use in this game from the TV version.

#2: Four performers stand in a row facing the audience. From stage right to stage left, let's refer to them as Player 1, Player 2, Player 3, and Player 4.

#3: Going from stage right to stage left, each of the performers sing one line. This starts with Player 1 and moves down the line until Player 4 has sung a line. Once four lines have been sung, that completes a round of the game.

#4: The aim is for the line sung by the Player 4 to rhyme with the line sung by the Player 2.

#5: Between rounds, the players all act like they're holding glasses of beer and sing a simple tune *(hi-di di-di di-di di-di di-di di-di-diiiii!)*

#6: In round two, the same pattern is repeated, except this time, the order of who sings when is shifted. The first line of round two is sung by Player 2, and it moves down the line so that the second line is sung by the Player 3, the third line sung by the Player 4, and the final line is now sung by Player 1.

#7: This repeats again for rounds three and four and each round is started by the next player in the line who hasn't started a round yet.

How Does the Game End?

After four rounds of the song.

Pro Tips:

Pro Tip #1: As the game is called Irish Drinking Song, it is optional if you wish to attempt doing an Irish accent during the game. This can add to the fun but isn't a requirement.

Pro Tip #2: If you are the second player to sing a line during a round, you will be giving the word that the fourth player has to rhyme with. As such, make this something simple and say it clearly to give them the best chance to hit that rhyme.

Pro Tip #3: Think about what the topic or theme for the song is. If you can, try to make the rhymes include words that relate to the theme. Doing this will get the best reaction from the audience in most cases.

Pro Tip #4: This game is played over four rounds, and gives you the opportunity to build something of a story throughout the song. Each round can be seen as a separate chapter of the story. It's not always possible, especially as there will be four people adding to the story, but if you can, try to progress the story to something new happening with each round.

88: WHOOPS...I DID IT AGAIN

Emcee Intro Script: It's time for a song! This will be a game for everyone, and in it, the performers are going to make up a song, but only the person that I *(The Emcee)* am pointing at will be allowed to continue the song. If they fail to pick up the song and continue the lyrics in a way that makes sense, or they hesitate or completely change the tune...they're out!

Challenge Style: Singing

Players: 4+

Ask the Audience For: The name of a song that doesn't actually exist.

Setup: This game can be played with backing music, or it can be played with no music in the background as it is quite stop start.

How to Play the Game:

#1: The players all stand in a line and the Emcee kneels down a few feet in front of them.

#2: Whoever the Emcee is pointing at has to continue the song for as long as the Emcee continues pointing at them.

#3: If the Emcee stops pointing at someone, that person must immediately stop singing, even if they are mid-sentence or mid-word.

#4: Whoever the Emcee points at next must continue the song from the exact point the other player stopped singing at.

#5: If a player fails to stop singing when they should, or doesn't continue singing from the previous player in a way that sounds like a continuation, they are eliminated from the game.

#6: If a player hesitates or mumbles, or the lyrics don't make sense, or they go drastically off tune, they are eliminated from the game.

#7: Every time a player is eliminated, the Emcee should get the eliminated player to step away from the line. The Emcee should then restart the game to repeat the process until there is only one player left. This player will be the winner of the game.

How Does the Game End?

It ends once all but one player is eliminated.

Pro Tips:

Pro Tip #1: Use a combination of faster and slower lyrics as you sing. If the lyrics are all very fast, it will be more difficult for the next player to continue from where you left off, but if everyone is too slow, it'll make the game seem too easy.

Pro Tip #2: Make sure you really listen to all of the other performers to see what the story of the song is. The song will sound better if it sounds like a real song, tells a story, and has repeating choruses.

Pro Tip #3: Don't back up sing. In other singing games, I'll advise performers that they can harmonise or sing along with others to support their fellow players. In this game, doing so will really make it unclear if people are coming in when they shouldn't.

Pro Tip #4: Make sure you pay attention to the Emcee. The Emcee will be the person pointing at the player who has to sing currently. If you are looking at the person who is currently singing, you may miss when you get pointed at.

Pro Tip #5: Be active. This is a singing game, and it'll enhance the game if it seems all performers are getting into it. You could do a little shuffle or dance on the spot, but still make sure you are watching the Emcee, and that you're also not pulling focus from the current singer. Any movement should be to support the other performers and not distract from them.

See Also: The original Extreme Improv Big Book of Improv Games includes a game called Story Story Die, which is also known as Whoops, and of which this is a singing variation. Please refer to the guide in that book for more information and tips that will help you play this game, and a similar non singing storytelling version.

SECTION 10: RECREATION GAMES

All the games in this section are about players recreating something.

All the games in this section are about players recreating something.

All the games in this section are about players recreating something.

All the games in this section are about players recreating something.

All the games in this section are about players recreating something.

You get the idea...

89: ONE MINUTE SEQUEL

Emcee Intro Script: We're going to do some One Minute Sequels to your favourite movies! You'll be able to see what the continuing adventures were of some of your favourite movies and characters.

And in this game one or two performers will have one minute to create the entire sequel. Not just one scene, but we'll effectively get a highlight reel of the entire movie that has never been seen before!

Challenge Style: Scene based

Players: 1+

Ask the Audience For: A famous film that hasn't had a sequel. For example, if the audience suggest Die Hard, there is already a Die Hard 2, so you could clarify that what you would present would be Die Hard 6 as *(at the time of writing)* there have been five Die Hard movies.

How to Play the Game:

#1: Whether there are one or two players in the game, the one/two players will take on multiple roles and play every character in the story.

#2: The players should quickly rush through all of the elements of what the sequel story would be. Don't just do one long scene, but try to create a sense of a full film's worth of story condensed into one minute. This means including a beginning, middle and end.

Using a made up sequel for Die Hard as an example:

The first ten seconds could show the main character John McClane visiting his daughter at Christmas.

After ten seconds you could notice a helicopter outside and have bad guys jump in through the window and start shooting and do a quick action sequence.

By thirty seconds, John and his old partner Al could decide they need to rescue John's daughter. A bad guy could then shoot at John and Al jumps in front of the bullet and gets killed.

By forty-five seconds John could declare 'now things are personal'. And demand the bad guys let his daughter go.

For the final fifteen seconds you could have a lot of shooting, say his catchphrase and in the last few seconds have the daughter say 'let's go home' to wrap things up. Badabing badaboom! Yippee Ki-Yay and you're done.

How Does the Game End?

At the end of the one minute timer.

Pro Tips:

Pro Tip #1: If you don't know the film you're tasked with making a sequel to, just do what you think the film should be based on the title. I would say that it's worth making it obvious that you don't know the film, and the audience will be more likely to understand or accept whatever it is that you then come up with.

Pro Tip #2: Use different accents and physicality to show when you are playing different characters.

Pro Tip #3: If you do know the film that you are creating a one minute sequel to, feel free to throw in references or lines of dialogue from the original film. This will highlight that you know the film and any fans of the film are more likely to get a kick out of what you have created.

See Also: This game is a variant on the game One Minute Remake which was featured in the first Extreme Improv Big Book of Improv Games. The fundamentals of this game and that game are the same, but please see the guide for that game for more tips that will help you develop how to play One Minute Sequel.

90: FORSOOTH

Emcee Intro Script: You know how a lot of modern movies are based on Shakespeare plays? The Lion King is Hamlet, 10 Things I Hate About You is based on the Taming of the Shrew, and West Side Story is based on Romeo and Juliet. Well, we're going to do things the other way around. We're going to perform modern cinema classics in the language of William Shakespeare and the Elizabethan period.

Challenge Style: Scene based

Players: 2+

Ask the Audience For: A well-known movie

How to Play the Game:

#1: The performers should start the scene and establish the characters that they are playing from the well-known movie.

#2: You'll want to keep the story and characters and settings as close to the original film as possible, but the idea is that you should aim to Shakespearean-ise everything. For example, if you take a film like The Avengers, you could rename the characters to Sir Iron Man, Lord Hulk, and the Lady Black Widow in mourning.

#3: You should also attempt to change up the language to be more Shakespearean. Here's some examples:

Hulk doth smash my lady.

'tis time the Avengers assemble most merrily.

Wherefore art the infinity stones?

Thor is as strong as the oak rooted deep in the Earth's embrace.

How Does the Game End?

The Emcee can decide when is a good point to end the scene based on how long it's been going and if the cast reach a good ending point.

Pro Tips:

Pro Tip #1: Speak in metaphors, use rhyming couplets and deliver soliloquies to the audience. Shakespearean tropes and conventions are something many people are familiar with on a superficial level, so go with what is obvious like using words such as thee or thou and you should be fine.

If you wish to up your game, I'd suggest working on this in rehearsal and pooling ideas from your cast of what people know or would expect from a Shakespeare performance. You can actually go quite in depth with the performance and language style of the era. If you're performing to a knowledgeable audience, the more you show off your command of performing Shakespeare, the more you will impress.

Pro Tip #2: Building off the last point, it's worth doing a little research to watch plays or even videos of Shakespeare's plays being performed to see what the physicality is for the era.

91: HALF LIFE

Emcee Intro Script: Our next game is called Half Life...but shouldn't be confused with the video game. The performers will start by creating a scene that lasts sixty seconds. After this, the performers are going to be given thirty seconds to recreate the original scene and fit the whole story into half the length of time as the original scene.

After that, they will be given just fifteen seconds to recreate it again, and then finally just seven seconds to fit what once was a one minute story into a now very short period of time.

Challenge Style: Scene based

Players: 2+

Ask the Audience For: A random word to inspire the scene.

How to Play the Game:

#1: Two players create a scene based on the audience suggestion. The scene will be timed and last one minute.

#2: At the end of one minute, the Emcee should end the scene, but now remind the audience that the performers are going to recreate the same scene, but fit all of what they just did into half the time.

#3: The performers should now recreate the scene they just did, but speed up everything to get it to condensed down into thirty seconds. This should include a combination of literally speeding up their voices and any physical actions, but also making selective cuts to the content to fit it in.

#4: This process will then repeat multiple times with the time allowance reducing in half each time.

How Does the Game End?

When the performers have finally created a seven or three second scene and it cannot be squeezed down anymore.

Pro Tips:

Pro Tip #1: Make sure the original version of the scene includes plenty of content. Lots of back and forth dialogue, and physical action. If not much happened during the first iteration of the scene, it'll make recreating it seem too easy and seeing it over and over won't feel very fun.

Pro Tip #2: Don't go crazy speed on the first recreation. If you speed things up too fast too quick, it won't give you anywhere to go for the second and third recreations.

Pro Tip #3: The more you recreate the scene, the more rushed and heightened you can make things. Don't worry about getting all the same emotion in there. By the end, you should give a sense of panic as you try to get the entire scene squeezed into almost no time.

92: NINETY SECOND BOXSET

Emcee Intro Script: Life is busy, so who has time to binge watch all the hundreds of different TV shows that get pumped out on TV and streaming services each year? Not me! Luckily, we're about to play Ninety Second Box Set! Two performers will get to recreate a whole box set of a TV show, play every part, and do the whole story...in just ninety seconds.

Challenge Style: Scene based

Players: 2

Ask the Audience For: A well-known TV show. Ideally this should be some kind of drama, or comedy that has multiple episodes or seasons.

I'd avoid doing a soap opera as there will be literally thousands of episodes and characters in something like that which may make it too vast as a challenge. But you could do a soap opera if you think the room would be happy for it to be done. Likewise, documentaries, reality TV and news and sports shows aren't the best type of TV show for this game, but they are still doable.

How to Play the Game:

#1: Once the performers have got the suggestion, start the timer and they should attempt to play every character from the TV show, and basically do a montage of all of the major episodes and storylines that people would associate with the show.

Unlike One Minute Remake games, where you take a two hour film and have to squash it into one minute, the challenge of condensing what may be dozens of episodes of a TV show into just ninety seconds is even more impossible.

As such, you won't be able to do a very accurate recreation. Instead, you should aim to create something of a highlight reel of memorable moments to give an overview of the story of the show.

How Does the Game End?

At the end of ninety seconds.

Pro Tips:

Pro Tip #1: It's unlikely that everyone will have seen all the episodes of all the TV shows that you may be tasked with recreating. With this in mind, you should really aim to recreate moments that would be most familiar to most people. It's a safer bet to go with what is obvious than to do a deep cut for the hardcore fans of a specific show.

Pro Tip #2: If you are familiar with the show you are tasked with recreating, you and your scene partner could quickly agree just to recreate a single season of the show. This would make the challenge more manageable.

SECTION 11: PHYSICAL

For performers who like to get physical in your scenes, these are games that will allow you to demonstrate your physical skills and body control.

You can do it! Kneel!

I'm doing my best. And my name isn't Neil...

93: HUMAN PROPS

Emcee Intro Script: We're going to play Human Props! Two players will perform a scene where they will need various props throughout. Unlike most of the scenes we do in the show tonight, our performers are not allowed to mime that they are holding props. Instead, we'll have another two players who will have to transform and become every other prop that is needed!

Challenge Style: Scene based/Physical

Players: 4

Ask the Audience For: A place of work or mission the characters must complete.

How to Play the Game:

#1: Two players perform the scene as characters, whilst another two performers wait on the sidelines ready to enter the scene and take on the form of any prop that the characters may need.

#2: Every time the Character Performers need any kind of prop, they should verbally make it clear what they need. Then one of the Prop Performers should enter the scene and do their best to take on the form of whatever prop is required.

#3: Throughout the scene, the Character Performers should find many excuses for the Prop Performers to take on different physical forms. This can be as oversized handheld objects like telephones or screwdrivers, or large objects such as cars or doors.

#4: The Prop Performers shouldn't talk or ever be sentient versions of the inanimate objects they are portraying. If they are playing a prop that would make noise, they can make that noise. For example, a chainsaw.

#5: Once a Character Performer is done using the prop, they should make it clear they are putting the prop down and discarding it. The

Prop Performer should then quickly return to the sides neutrally to await the next time they are called upon.

How Does the Game End?

When the Emcee feels the scene has been explored enough.

Pro Tips:

Pro Tip #1: The fun of the game is seeing the Prop Performers having to reshape themselves to become various props. An aspect of the humour comes from seeing the performers giving up an element of their dignity to play such silly things such as a toilet roll or a garbage can.

Pro Tip #2: The Character Performers in the scene can have fun by making the Prop Performers have to take on the role of undesirable to play props. Look for opportunities to tease that you may need a toilet brush or such like, even if you don't end up going forward with it.

94: THE GORO GAME

Emcee Intro Script: In this game two players will work together to become one strange four-armed creature. These extra arms frequently seem as if they have a mind of their own and may or may not co-operate with the rest of their body.

Challenge Style: Scene based/Physical

Players: 2-4

Ask the Audience For: Something the characters are demonstrating. This may be dictated by props you have prepared for the show.

Setup:

#1: If possible, you could create special large T-shirts which each have four arm holes, and are large enough to fit two people inside. One player would stand behind the other and put their arms through under the arm pits of the player in front.

#2: If you are able to, this scene would also benefit from having a table with a variety of props on.

How to Play the Game:

#1: Two players will work together to create a single four-armed character. Player 1 will take on the main part of the character who we will refer to as the Face Character. They will still be able to use their full body and arms within the scene.

Player 2 will be referred to as the Extra Arms Character and will tuck their arms underneath the armpits of the Face Character performer to provide two additional arms. To get the positioning correct, it will be like the secondary performer is stood behind the Face Character and giving them a hug with their arms sticking out in front.

#2: The Face Character will lead the scene and be able to interact with other characters and any physical objects you have in the scene. Meanwhile, the Extra Arms performer will also be able to use their hands to interact with any objects, as well as other characters or the rest of the Face Character performer.

#3: Throughout the scene, you'll want to find ways to have the Extra Arms cause mischief. This may be something the Face Character is used to, or it may be that they are aware that their extra arms are an annoyance and problem.

How Does the Game End?

The Emcee should look for a suitable ending point to the game.

Pro Tips:

Pro Tip #1: The Extra Arms can and should somewhat have a mind of their own. If you understand this point of reference, the additional arms will behave something like the mechanical tentacles of the Spider-Man villain Doctor Octopus. It may be fun for the Face Character to have to continually keep the Extra Arms in check, and there be a sense that this character's arms are squabbling with each other.

Pro Tip #2: The action of the Extra Arms could be led by the person playing the Face Character, in that they verbally cue the arms. Or it could be that they physically lead the arms by handing things to them.

Alternatively, what the Extra Arms do could be entirely up to the Extra Arms performer. Ideally there should be an element of both involved.

Pro Tip #3: Think about what unique opportunities you have to use these extra arms in the scene. What would you do if you had an extra set of arms and hands to get more done. How would this improve your ability to play the piano, write a book, or eat with two sets of knives and forks at the same time.

Note: Its worth mentioning that this game does require some performers to work extremely closely together. Before throwing any two random performers into a game like this, it may be worth workshopping it in rehearsal to make sure people know what your boundaries are.

95: THEMED EXERCISES

Emcee Intro Script: It's time to make the performers sweat! Because we're going to play Themed Exercises! One of the performers is going to take on the role of a Gym Instructor and teach everyone else some exercises based on a theme of your choice! This could be something like The Zoo Routine where all the exercises are based on animals, or Office Aerobics where the workout is based on filing papers and having affairs with your co-workers!

Challenge Style: Physical

Players: 3+

Ask the Audience For: A theme such as a place of work or profession.

Setup: This game would benefit from having some low volume exercise warm up music in the background.

How to Play the Game:

#1: The player acting as the Gym Instructor should stand down stage centre and deliver this workout routine as if they are performing to be seen by the audience. You could speak to the audience as if they are watching you in a theatre, or you could speak to them as if they were watching you on a workout video.

#2: The other players should stand in some kind of formation behind and to the sides of the Gym Instructor. They should attempt to follow the lead of the Gym Instructor and copy the workout routines that the Gym Instructor demonstrates.

#3: As the exercise demonstration is going on, the Gym Instructor should narrate what they are doing. This should be to give advice and instructions to the other performers of why they should be doing the routines and how they will benefit from it.

#4: The method and techniques that the Gym Instructor are demonstrating should be inspired by the theme suggested by the audience. For example, if the theme was playing video games, all the exercises should in some way link to the activity of video games. It may be that one exercise is pretending to throw barrels like Donkey Kong, or another is doing wide claps of the hands to emulate the way Pac-Man eats power pellets.

How Does the Game End?

The game can be ended by the performer playing the Gym Instructor. Once they have finished doing all the exercises, they should announce that is the end of the workout.

Pro Tips:

Pro Tip #1: Be very physical throughout the game, but also don't forget to talk lots too if you are playing the Gym Instructor. Perform as an upbeat and motivational speaking character, and explain all of your inspirations for why you developed these exercises.

Pro Tip #2: You do have the option to get some of the audience to join in with the workout routine. This can either be from their seat in the audience, or you could get volunteers to join you on stage.

96: SUPER POSEDOWN

Emcee Intro Script: It's time for the Super Posedown! Inspired by the competitive posing competitions you get in the world of body building; our performers are going to instead flex their creative muscles with poses inspired by suggestions of anything the audience can imagine.

Challenge Style: Physical

Players: 2+

Ask the Audience For: Random words, but things like professions, sports, activities, animals or objects work best.

How to Play the Game:

#1: The players should form a line facing towards the audience. They should also have a little space between each performer, so they have room to create their poses.

#2: The Emcee should ask for a different suggestion of word for each round.

#3: Once a suggestion has been gathered, the performers should be given a few seconds to do their pose. Treat getting into pose as part of the performance.

#4: The poses should be inspired by whatever the audience suggestion was. So, if the suggestion was *'doctor'* you may want to pose like you're doing surgery or chest compressions. If you have to pose like an animal, you should strike a pose which suggests that animal's stance and behaviour.

#5: When the performers do each pose, the Emcee should encourage applause as if they have just done something incredible.

#6: The Emcee should then get the audience to vote on who did the winning pose.

#7: This process can be repeated for multiple rounds.

How Does the Game End?

When the Emcee gets the votes of the final round.

Pro Tips:

Pro Tip #1: Even though the game has nothing to do with body building, I'd suggest the players perform it in a similar style to actual body building posedowns. Your persona in the game should be of someone who is taking the competition seriously, and you can stretch and flex to prepare for each pose.

Pro Tip #2: Don't forget that you can use facial expressions and limited amounts of sounds to enhance your pose. When it comes to speech, you could just use a single word growled through your pose to sum up what you are doing, or maybe you could use an element of smack talk to say why you are the best.

97: THE SHOW MUST GO ON

Emcee Intro Script: In our next game, the performers will start a scene as if they are performing in a play. But every forty-five seconds or so, one of the cast will unexpectedly die. In the spirit that the Show Must Go On, the others will have to keep going without acknowledging that the cast are slowly dying off. This means that the remaining living players have to help their fallen comrades to keep moving and talking so the scene can keep going.

Challenge Style: Scene based

Players: 4+

Ask the Audience For: A title for the fictional play

How to Play the Game:

#1: All the performers involved begin a scene and establish the story of the play.

#2: After forty-five seconds, the Emcee should call *'die'* or press a buzzer/bell to signify that one of the cast has to die. They could also point at or name the player who is next to die.

#3: The way the performer dies is up to them. It could just be that they suddenly collapse, or they could demonstrate some kind of mishap within the context of what they're doing in the scene. Either way, it should be obvious that the character wasn't meant to die as part of the ongoing play.

#4: It'll now be the responsibility of the remaining cast to keep the show going without acknowledging that one of the cast members just died. To do this, the remaining cast members should pick up the "dead" actor and move them about the stage to do whatever it was that they would have done if they hadn't died.

This will include moving their mouth and saying words for them like they are a puppet, as well as moving their arms and hands to give the sense that they're still alive and playing their part.

#5: The Emcee should repeat the process every forty-five seconds, and another cast member should die at these intervals. Once again, whoever is left will have to do their best to continue the story and speak for, and move everyone else.

How Does the Game End?

The game ends once the final cast member dies.

Pro Tips:

Pro Tip #1: This game has the aspect of each performer playing the dual role of the character in the scene and also playing the performer who is playing the character.

As such, you can have fun with the idea of watching your cast mates die one by one. How does this affect you? This may add a sense of panic or fear, but this shouldn't stop your main goal that the show must go on.

Pro Tip #2: Performers playing dead bodies should slump their heads to one side, have their eyes shut, and be very floppy in their bodies and limbs. At times you will need to be helpful to the performers who are trying to puppet you.

So, if you are dead on the ground, and one of the living characters tries to pick you up to walk across the stage, you should just get up and walk to the right position as they guide you. It may be funny to occasionally go limp if they let go of you, but it would also be ok for you to play dead but play dead whilst being stood up.

SECTION 12: PROPS/TECH REQUIRED

Here's a variety of games which require something else beyond the performers themselves. Most games in this book can be jumped into wherever you are, but for these ones you may need some kind of technical requirement or prop to get going.

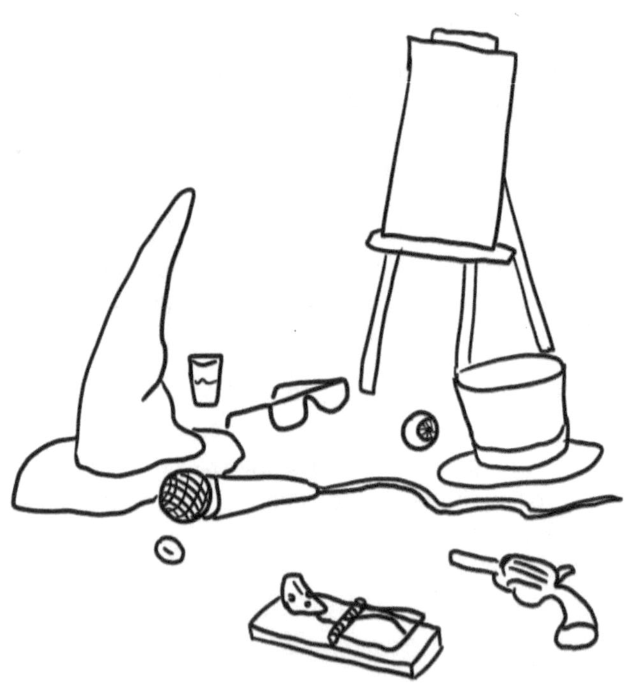

Improv is like the ultimate hidden object game because usually they're all invisible!

98: MOUSETRAPS AND LEGOS

Emcee Intro Script: Warning. This game may hurt! We're going to play Mousetraps and Legos. In it, our performers will be blindfolded and have to complete the scene as if they can see. But that's not all. The stage will be covered in mousetraps. But that's not all. In between the mousetraps will be Lego bricks. And that still isn't all. They'll have to take their shoes and socks off before they begin.

Warning: Whilst versions of this game have been played by prominent improv performers and even aired on television, I will warn most people against playing it. As many a parent will know, stepping onto a toy Lego brick *(or cheap knock off equivalent)* can really hurt. Likewise, if you were to catch yourself in a mousetrap, it would also hurt and could lead to injury.

You can get toy mousetraps which look the part but wouldn't cause serious injury such as broken toes etc. However, I would only suggest this game to be played by professional performers who use rigged props that will be visually effective, but are safe to use.

Challenge Style: Scene based

Players: 2

Ask the Audience For: Something the characters are searching for.

Setup: Before the game is started the players should be blindfolded, remove their shoes, and mousetraps and Lego bricks should be scattered over the playing area.

How to Play the Game:

#1: The players are blindfolded and placed opposite sides of the stage.

#2: The Emcee *(and helpers)* then place mousetraps and Lego bricks, scattered onto the performance area.

#3: The performers should now be instructed to remove their shoes and socks.

#4: The players can now begin the scene, where they are encouraged to continuously keep moving about the performance area. The performers should perform the scene as if they can see, despite their blindfolds.

#5: As the performers move about, they are likely to step on either the mousetraps or the Lego bricks. As they do this, it is likely to be painful for the performers and they should respond accordingly to highlight their pain.

As mentioned in the warning earlier, I would suggest this game be played with rigged mousetraps that wouldn't really hurt, and don't have enough built in force to actually break any bones.

The idea of the game is for the audience to laugh at the performers expense for what is essentially an improvised slapstick routine. It's likely that even with rigged mousetraps, the shock of any traps snapping down are likely to make the performers jump and yell out. I would suggest you be truthful to what your reactions are, and not purposely overreact, as otherwise, the audience are less likely to believe that they hurt at all.

How Does the Game End?

The Emcee should call scene once the players have activated several of the traps and the scene has gone on for a decent length of time.

Pro Tips:

Pro Tip #1: A lot of the fun for the audience will come from the sense of anticipation of you stepping on something painful. Use a mix of walking very small steps to avoid stepping on the traps, and doing large over the top steps as if to step over them. Inevitably this will mean you end up stepping on some.

Pro Tip #2: Something I certainly wouldn't recommend you do often, but which could prove very funny, would be if a player ended up on the floor amongst the traps. This could happen if stepping on a trap was to make someone go to their knees, or if someone was to fall down. This scenario would probably see many traps activated in quick succession, and would create a funny ending to the game.

99: TOTALLY SKETCHY

Emcee Intro Script: This next game is totally sketchy…which is quite handy as it is called Totally Sketchy too. In it, our players will be tasked with presenting an art based show.

Challenge Style: Art based

Players: 1+

Ask the Audience For: A volunteer who would like their portrait drawn.

Setup: For each player taking part in this game, you will need a large sketch pad and some marker pens. Ideally, you'll also need an easel to put the sketch pad on so the audience can see the drawings as they are being done. An alternative could be to use a white board and dry marker pens, but it may be nice to use a sketch pad as the audience member could take home their portrait.

How to Play the Game:

#1: Ask for an audience member to join you on stage and position them *(ideally sat on a chair)* so that the player/players drawing them can clearly see the volunteer.

#2: The player/s doing the drawing should talk the audience through their artistic process as they draw the audience member and also engage the volunteer in light banter.

How Does the Game End?

This whole game should last three to five minutes, which should be plenty of time for the player to have drawn the audience member. The Emcee can interrupt at any point if the picture is complete early or if they feel the scene is losing steam.

If two players or more are doing drawings it would be recommended to ask the audience to vote on which piece of art they prefer, to decide a winner. It may also be worth noting that tastes in art are entirely subjective.

Pro Tips:

Pro Tip #1: Whether the players drawing are good or bad at art, the aim shouldn't be to insult or upset the audience member. Caricatures are fine, but be careful to not purposely insult the volunteer.

Pro Tip #2: It can be fun to purposely invent details on the picture being drawn. This could be that you do a drawing of the audience member, but change their costume in the picture to depict them slaying a dragon, or working in a specific job, or at an unexpected location. Inspiration for this could come from your own imagination, or they could be ideas that come from banter with the audience members during the scene.

100: HATS

Emcee Intro Script: Our next game is Hats! Players will take turns to step forward whilst wearing different hats to play lots of different characters. This is a quick-fire game, and the performers will be playing examples of the worst imaginable examples of a type of person you suggest.

Challenge Style: Quick fire

Players: 2+

Ask the Audience For: A suggestion of a job that the characters are applying for.

Alternatively, the Emcee can instead be the one to suggest specific types of characters the performers would be playing. For example, *the person you wouldn't like to move in next door*, or *the worst person to see on a dating video.*

Setup: You should prepare one or two large boxes that can be filled with many different types of hats, wigs and masks.

How to Play the Game:

#1: The players should rummage through the hats to find one that inspires an idea that they can present to the audience.

#2: Once a hat has been selected, the players should take turns to step forward and speak one or two lines of dialogue which relates to a character choice that their hat/wig/mask would suggest.

#3: In terms of what you say, you'll most likely want to come up with puns that link to the hats, but you could make other types of jokes or use observational humour.

Different types of hats: Here's some suggestions for the types of hats you could use in the game. Cowboy hat, space helmet, French beret, fez, baseball cap with helicopter blades, crown, wizard hat, sailor hat, Batman mask, lucha mask, mad scientist wig.

How Does the Game End?

Either once the performers have run out of hats/wigs etc, or whilst there are still a few left. It's better to leave the audience wanting to see more rather than you use up all the hats just to have used them all.

Pro Tips:

Pro Tip #1: The easiest jokes to get out of the game are puns. So, for example, if you were wearing a space helmet and the scenario was that you were doing a dating video, you could step forward and say *'one day, I hope we get married and have a Sun'*. Things like this are easy to generate based on the hat type.

The force is backwards with this one

101: LEFT OVER LINES

Emcee Intro Script: Our next game is called Left Over Lines, and is a game for one performer. Using lines of dialogue written by the audience, the player will incorporate these into a monologue they are about to create. It's their job to make these lines make sense within the context of the monologue they are performing.

See Also: This game can be played in its own right, but is an excellent companion game to happen later within a show where you have played the game Whose Line. The idea would be that you play Whose Line as a two or three hander, and then later in the show, you give one player the Left Over Lines not used in the earlier game. Hence the name Left Over Lines. The details of how to play the game Whose Line was detailed in the first Extreme Improv Big Book of Improv Games.

Challenge Style: Monologue

Players: 1

Setup: Before the show starts, ask the audience to write short lines of dialogue onto slips of paper to use in the show. A good way to ask for this is to hand each audience member a piece of paper and a pen as they enter. Or you can have a cast member/helper go around and hand these out as they are waiting for the show to begin.

Ask the Audience For: When it comes to playing the game, ask the audience for a theme for a dramatic monologue.

How to Play the Game:

#1: The player should begin the monologue to establish who they are and what is on their character's mind.

#2: I would suggest that the performer has a pile of the Left Over Lines in their hand or in a pocket.

#3: Every so often, the player should read one of the lines of dialogue as if it is part of the speech they are already saying. The idea is that the written line is incorporated as if it is part of the speech and not that the character is reading something aloud.

#4: Once you have said the line of dialogue you should justify how it fits into the monologue and continue to integrate the ideas of it into the continuing speech.

How Does the Game End?

When the performer brings the monologue to an end. They should try to find a suitable ending themselves, but the Emcee could also end it, if they don't.

Pro Tips:

Pro Tip #1: You may find that some of the lines of dialogue written by the audience don't gel well with the theme of what you're talking about. A good way to overcome this is to set up that you're about to read one of the lines, by framing it as a quote from someone. For example, you could say the following:

This reminds me of what my father told me on my birthday...(followed by the line from the audience)

Or

I must remember that...(read the audience suggestion)

In these examples you would still have to justify whatever the audience suggested line was but this gives more wiggle room for the lines not sounding a natural part of the speech.

Pro Tip #2: Don't read the lines to yourself before you say them out loud in front of the audience. At most I would suggest you take a split second to make sure that the line doesn't contain anything inappropriate or offensive. Otherwise, just read it aloud as the lines will lose some impact if it seems you've had time to prepare/filter or edit what you're saying. A cold read will likely end up feeling the most spontaneous and funny.

102: SOUND EFFECTS

Emcee Intro Script: We're going to play Sound Effects! There will be two performers in the scene who will talk and move about. These will be our Scene Performers. Then, there will be two Sound Performers who will provide the sound effects for anything in the scene other than speech.

Challenge Style: Scene based

Players: 4

Ask the Audience For: Where the characters are or what they are doing.

Note: The Sound Performers could be two audience members rather than other cast members.

Setup: Ideally, you'll need microphones for the Sound Performers.

How to Play the Game:

#1: Before you begin, the Emcee should instruct the Sound Performers as to who they are providing sound effects for. Each of the Sound Performers should be told to make sound effects for only one Scene Performer each.

#2: The two Scene Performers create a scene on the stage and establish their characters and the scenario.

#3: Along the way, the Scene Performers should set up opportunities for sound effects to be required. This can be done by miming using objects such as a chainsaw, electric toothbrush, opening doors, ringing a doorbell etc.

It is worth the Scene Performers sign posting what sound effect they're expecting with dialogue. For example:

Scene Performer 1: *Let me just start this chainsaw...*

Sound Performer 1: *(makes a sound like a chainsaw)*

#4: The Sound Performers should stand to one side of the stage so they can see the scene unfold.

When it is apparent that a sound effect is needed, the Sound Performers should do their best to make the sound into the microphone. The Scene Performers should react as if the sounds have come from within their environment.

#5: The Sound Performers don't always have to wait for the Scene Performers to indicate that they need a sound made.

The Sound Performers could be proactive in making sounds like a phone ringing, or the wind blowing if they think it fits.

How Does the Game End?

At the discretion of the Emcee.

Pro Tips:

Pro Tip #1: You can have a lot of fun playing with expectations in this game. For example, let's say one of the Scene Performers sets up that they are using a chainsaw.

If the sound provided by the Sound Performer sounds weak or weird, it won't match the audience's expectations of what a chainsaw should sound like. This would likely get a laugh. The Scene Performer can then comment on the chainsaw not working as expected.

Pro Tip #2: The Scene Performers have the opportunity to speak in such a way as to provide commentary on how the Sound Performers are doing at providing sounds. If done well, they should be able to do this without actually breaking character.

In a sense this is breaking the fourth wall, but actually, it's more like blurring the fourth wall. The Scene Performers shouldn't fully come out of character to say *'that sound effect was weird'* but instead with a nod and wink to the audience stay in character and say *'I guess the chainsaw is broken.'* This is a fun way to highlight if the sound effects are or are not very well performed.

Pro Tip #3: If you use volunteers from the audience as the Sound Performers, they may need encouragement from the Emcee or from the Scene Performers to give more or bigger sounds if they are on the backfoot. Usually, the Scene Performers can do this whilst staying in character.

For example, if a chainsaw noise was not very loud, a Scene Performer could announce that they're going to *really rev it this time, and that it might get loud!'*

Doing this will indicate to the volunteer Sound Performer what is expected. The good news is that if they do it loud, you've got what you wanted, and if they do it quietly again, it'll probably be funny.

Pro Tip #4: Realistically, if you use volunteers from the audience as the Sound Performers, they are less likely to be as proactive in making sounds on their own, so don't expect them to lead with any sounds.

See Also: The original Extreme Improv Big Book of Improv Games has the game Sound FX, which is similar to this, but played without speech and only one active player in the game. For some reason, both games are regularly called either Sound Effects or Sound FX, so you are likely to encounter either with the other version of the name.

103: PICTURE PERFECT

Emcee Intro Script: We are going to play Picture Perfect! This is a game for two players. They will create a scene, but every line of dialogue they say will be influenced by a random image that we will display on the projector.

Challenge Style: Scene based

Players: 2

Ask the Audience For: Where the characters are or what they are doing.

Setup: For this game you'll need a projector. You'll also need to prepare many random images to display. These can either be displayed randomly, if you are able to, or they can be put into a slide show.

How to Play the Game:

#1: Two players start a scene.

#2: Before every line of dialogue is said, a new random image should be displayed on a projector that both the performers and audience can see.

#3: Each line of dialogue that is said by a performer should be influenced by what the picture is. Here are some examples of ways that lines of dialogue could be influenced by images:

Image of apple: *You are the apple of my eye.*

Image of someone falling over: *I think I've fallen in love with you.*

Image of tree: *I went to my local bank branch.*

#4: After every line has been said by a performer, the Emcee/Tech should change the image to a new one to inspire the next line of dialogue.

#5: The scene should not just be a collection of random lines. The aim is to continue to build a scene with a progressing story.

How Does the Game End?

When the Emcee has had the players go through lots of images.

Pro Tips:

Pro Tip #1: Be careful not to spend the whole scene looking at the projections. You should still interact and engage with your scene partner and make sure your body and face are visible for the audience.

Try to angle your body so that you can be seen by the audience and quickly look to the projections to get inspiration for the next line.

Pro Tip #2: Don't acknowledge the images on the projections as being images you are looking at within the context of the scene you are creating. The idea is that your conversation is happening, and that you are not actually seeing the images as your character.

SECTION 13: STORYTELLING

It's story time with Extreme Improv bay bay! Here are a selection of games for the storytellers among us. Get ready to settle down with a cup of tea and a nice biscuit as we tell you some fabulous stories which will all be made up on the spot.

Once upon a time, there was an improviser and an audience member. The audience member got very suggestive...

104: TWO WORDS AT A TIME STORY

Emcee Intro Script: We're now going to have a Two Word at a Time Story! Our performers are going to create a story together, and they are going to each contribute two words at a time.

Challenge Style: Storytelling

Players: 3+

Ask the Audience For: A theme for a story

How to Play the Game:

#1: All the players in the game should stand in a line facing the audience. From stage right to stage left, let's say there is Player 1, Player 2, Player 3 and Player 4.

#2: Starting with the player furthest to stage right, which is Player 1, they should begin to tell a story where each player adds two words at a time to it. For example:

Player 1: *One day...*

Player 2: *a man...*

Player 3: *found his...*

Player 1: *true love...*

Player 2: *in prison...*

How Does the Game End?

When the Emcee feels the story has either reached a suitable ending, or the story has run out of steam. It is possible that the players can end it themselves. If they reach an ending, the next player to speak could simply say *'the end'*.

Pro Tips:

Pro Tip #1: Try to make the story flow without stopping for pauses between each player's speech. One thing that can go towards achieving this is picking up on, and continuing the emotion said by the previous player.

Pro Tip #2: Avoid announcing punctuation like saying *'full stop.'* You should be able to hear when new sentences begin without having to announce that a sentence has ended.

See Also: The Extreme Improv Big Book of Improv Games features the game Word at a Time Story which is a one word at a time version of this.

Variants: As well as one word and two words at a time story games, you could take this up to three or four words at a time. I would suggest three is probably the maximum you'd want to do though as doing more will become harder for the players to keep track of.

Wasn't quite what we meant by two words at a time...

105: GROUP POEM

Emcee Intro Script: We're now going to create a poem for you, and we're going to do it as a group. That's right. We're playing Group Poem!

Challenge Style: Storytelling/Poetry

Players: 2+

Ask the Audience For: A theme for the poem, or a title of the poem.

How to Play the Game:

#1: For this example, let's say there are five people taking part in the group poem. For best results, the players should stand in a line, or another formation. If you are not in an obvious line, be certain that you know the order that the players are going to speak.

#2: Player 1 will start the poem by saying one opening line.

#3: Player 2 then does two lines. Player 2's first line has to rhyme with the opening line from Player 1. Player 2's second line should set up what Player 3 has to rhyme with.

#4: This process continues with all additional players.

For example:

Player 1: *I will say one opening line!*

Player 2: *Which is a great start and is mighty fine,*

    But then the second gets not one, but two,

Player 3: *And the same for me, that's also true!*

    Every next player gets two and not three,

Player 4: *As we now demonstrate for you to see,*

    I'm the fourth and what am I good for?

Player 5: *I'll take the fifth and not say more,*

    Because this poem is almost done

Player 1: *And returns to one line to end on player one!*

In the example given, every player has two lines each, which they say back-to-back with the exception of Player 1.

Player 1 gives a single opening line, and the poem ends on them closing the poem with a single closing line.

Despite this example, you could choose to continue for a second or third round to have a longer poem. If you do continue it for multiple rounds, then Player 1 would of course say two lines back-to-back as the other players do after their opening line. That is, until the final line.

How Does the Game End?

Once the players have reached some kind of end in the poem. This doesn't have to end with any player in particular, but when the Emcee recognises that an ending line has been reached.

The Emcee should interject and call *'and scene'* to solidify that the game has ended so that the other players don't attempt for it to continue.

Pro Tips:

Pro Tip #1: Don't intentionally end your lines with hard to rhyme with words. This can be funny to do, but unless you're very confident that the following players are going to cope with tricky words, it is better to give words that will be easier to rhyme with.

Pro Tip #2: Make sure you really listen to all the other players so that you can contribute to the story and build it up.

106: ONE WORD SAYS IT ALL

Emcee Intro Script: They say a picture speaks a thousand words. In this game, we'll see if one word can speak a thousand pictures. In a moment we'll ask you for suggestions of stories. Then our performers will step forward and create that story with just a single word backed up by all their acting ability and true emotion.

Challenge Style: Storytelling

Players: 1+

Ask the Audience For: A suggestion of what the story is about. This can either be a well-known story, something personal or something original.

How to Play the Game:

#1: Players stand in a line, and step forward either individually or together to create the story. They can take anywhere from five to thirty seconds to say the one word that tells their story.

For example, if the theme given is *'death'* a player could step forward and mime pulling a grenade pin and dropping the grenade. Their one word could then be *'whoops'*.

Another example may be that the theme is *'regret'*. The player could simply step forward and say *'marriage'*. The way they sell the word and react afterwards will be what connects the dots for the audience to understand what their intention with the word may be.

How Does the Game End?

Once the players have created several single word stories

Pro Tips:

Pro Tip #1: This game can be challenging if it's deemed that your word doesn't satisfy that it has told the story. Don't drag things out before saying your word unless you're confident that the payoff will be worth the build-up. Thirty seconds can be a long time for a game like this.

107: TWO LINE HORROR STORY

Emcee Intro Script: It's going to get spooky now, as our next game is Two Line Horror Story. The players will step forward to make up horror stories that are only two lines long.

Challenge Style: Quick Fire/Storytelling

Players: 1+

Ask the Audience For: Themes for the horror stories. These can be locations, objects or types of monsters. I would suggest asking for a variety and mixing it up here or there.

How to Play the Game:

#1: Once the suggestion is given by the audience, the player who is going to tell the story should step forward to deliver their version of the story.

#2: The stories should be two lines in length, but you'll get away with it if the story is just one line or ends up as three or four lines. If it goes more than four short lines in length, it'll probably seem too long for what the game promises to be.

#3: The stories can be simple, but they are best if you can incorporate some kind of twist into them. Here are some examples of both simple and twist based stories that have the theme of 'food'.

Simple: *I cooked the family meal. They didn't know it was poisoned.*

With a twist: *I had my friend for dinner. He was delicious.*

How Does the Game End?

Once several stories have been told.

Pro Tips:

Pro Tip #1: Adding twists work in a similar way to coming up with punchlines in a lot of the joke telling games in this book.

A good way to seek a good twist is to use word play and double meanings. For example:

At the restaurant, he gave him the stake...straight into the vampire's heart.

This story works on the idea that a stake, as in a wooden stake that would be used to kill a vampire, sounds the same as the word steak, as in a beef steak.

By establishing that the story is set within a restaurant it will lead the audience to believe that the stake is in fact an edible steak. Therefore, the audience wouldn't expect the twist of it being a wooden stake to kill a vampire.

Pro Tip #2: Whether you have a great story or a weaker one, you can often present them to the audience as being better than they are by saying them in an atmospheric or creepy voice.

Did you hear about the Werewolf?

It was all over the silver bulletin

108: STORY CASCADE

Emcee Intro Script: It's story time! The performers are going to make up a story, but they will be restricted how many words they can add to the story at a time. The first player who starts the story will add just one word, the second will add two, the third three, the fourth four...etc

Challenge Style: Storytelling

Players: 3+

Ask the Audience For: Something that the story may be about

Setup: The players should stand in a line across the stage and face the audience.

How to Play the Game:

There are two versions of this game. Let's explore both as if there are four players taking part.

Version #1: In the first version of this game, Player 1 would always add one word to the story at a time, Player 2 would always add two words at a time, Player 3 would always add three words at a time, and Player 4 would always add four words to the story at a time.

Once Player 4 has added their words, the next player to speak would be Player 1, who would once again add just one word to the story.

Version #2: This version is slightly more complicated to explain but is still essentially played the same way.

The order the players speak will always be Player 1, Player 2, Player 3, Player 4. This order never changes.

The difference comes in how many words are added with each turn. On version 2, the number of words added continually increases and decreases in a cascading wave. It initially goes one, two, three, four. Then decreases back three, two, one. Before going back up two, three, four. This pattern continues throughout the game.

This is easier in practice than it is to try to explain on paper, so here is an example game that should make it clearer:

Example Game:

Player 1: *Today* (adds one word)

Player 2: *there was* (adds two words)

Player 3: *a great big* (adds three words)

Player 4: *explosion outside the studio* (adds four words)

Player 1: *it was so* (adds three words)

Player 2: *loud that* (adds two words)

Player 3: *everyone* (adds one word)

Player 4: *ran away* (adds two words)

Player 1: *and hid in* (adds three words)

Player 2: *their houses never to* (adds four words)

Player 3: *be seen again.* (adds three words)

Player 4: *The end.* (adds two words)

How Does the Game End?

The players can bring the story to a natural conclusion at any stage.

Pro Tips:

Pro Tip #1: As with other story based games where players take turns to add set numbers of words, be careful to listen to the story being developed. Keeping continuity will be a group effort, so if you just say any random word, it may contradict what has already been established if you're not careful.

Pro Tip #2: Allow there to be natural full stops in the story. Avoid continually saying connecting words like *'and'* or *'but'* or *'because'* that never let a sentence end.

SECTION 14: GUESSING GAMES

What types of games could these be? That's right...they're all ones where there is a mystery element that will require detective work to figure out.

No, I'm not Mr E! How dare you question Mark!

109: IMPRESSION OVERLOAD

Emcee Intro Script: We're now going to play Impression Overload! One player is going to be given a list of fictional characters or well-known people that they will have to do impressions of. The other players are going to have to guess who the impressions are of.

It goes without saying that the player doing the impressions isn't allowed to say the name of their character, and they're not allowed to do other sneaky tactics like saying *'my name rhymes with…'*

Challenge Style: Guessing Game

Players: 2+

Ask the Audience For: You can ask the audience to write down the names of characters or well-known people on slips of paper to be used in this game. Do this before the show begins, or during an interval.

How to Play the Game:

#1: Player 1 is provided with a list or stack of cue cards/slips of paper where each one has a different character name on it.

#2: Each player has one minute *(or ninety second)* to perform as many of these impressions as possible.

#3: Other players, *(or the audience)* then have to guess as many of these as they can within the set time limit.

#4: If the player doing the impressions doesn't know how to do the impression, or the people guessing are very stuck, the player doing the impressions can call out *'Skip'* to show that they are moving onto a different impression.

Variations: This game can be played as a single player doing impressions and the others having to guess. Alternatively, it can be played as two teams where only their teammates can guess and try to get a higher score. Lastly, it can be played that every player takes turns to do impressions.

If every player takes turns to do impressions, I suggest that scoring works as follows: For every character guessed, both the player who guessed correctly and the player doing the impressions score a point. This prevents tactics such as Guessing Players purposely not guessing a character correctly to waste time and prevent the person doing impressions scoring points.

How Does the Game End?

The game ends when all of the players have taken their turn.

Pro Tips:

Pro Tip #1: If doing impressions, do your best to imitate the character's voice or their physicality, or quote things they are well known for saying.

If you don't think you know the character well enough to do any of these, you can go the route of vaguely describing yourself in character.

For example, if you were Harry Potter and didn't really know what the character does or what they sound like, you could say *'ooh let me just put my glasses on, and hope my scruffy hair covers my lightning bolt scar...'*

Pro Tip #2: Don't worry if you can't do good impressions. Some players feel nervous over doing impressions or accents, but if you purposely do them over the top, you'll usually get a laugh for your attempt.

Pro Tip #3: Some players don't feel comfortable doing impressions of people who come from different backgrounds such as different accents, ethnicities or genders to what they are.

This is something you should discuss in rehearsals before you play the game and work out what player's comfort levels are. For the most part I feel that if impressions are done with good intentions and not done to mock others, most impressions can be attempted by any player. You can always choose to skip a character and acknowledge *'I probably shouldn't do that impression'* if you think it wouldn't be suitable or appropriate.

110: DATING GAME

Emcee Intro Script: It's time for the Dating Game! In this game one of our performers will have the opportunity to meet their dream date! The other players will play their prospective dates, but they each have an unusual quirk that will have to be guessed.

Challenge Style: Guessing Game

Players: 3+

Ask the Audience For: Either ask the audience for suggestions of what the Dating Contestants quirks should be, or these can be provided by the Emcee. Ideally you will want the audience to know what the quirks are before the game begins so they are in on the joke. To achieve this, feel free to ask the Guessing Player to leave the room or wear headphones to block sound as these are announced.

How to Play the Game:

#1: The stage should be divided into two areas. The Guessing Player should sit on a chair stage right with the other players sat on chairs in a row stage left as the Dating Contestants. The idea is to create the look of a TV Dating Show. If you have a dividing wall that you can use this will add to the look but isn't required for the game to work.

#2: The Guessing Player should ask the Dating Contestants questions that would be typical on a dating show. Questions about where they would go on a date, or what their hobbies are etc.

#3: The Dating Contestants should answer the Guessing Player's questions in ways to give clues to what their quirks are. These answers should still fit the theme of being on a dating show but should also demonstrate their specific quirks.

For example, let's say Dating Contestant Number 1's quirk is that they are a retired boxer. They could answer questions about a relationship by saying that *'they look forward to showing their footwork on the dance floor and letting their guard down. And that maybe within time there may be a ring involved.'*

How Does the Game End?

Once the Guessing Player has asked each Dating Contestant two or three questions, the Emcee should encourage the Guessing Player to guess what the Dating Contestant's quirks are.

Pro Tips:

Pro Tip #1: If you are one of the Dating Contestants you should try to make your clues to your quirk subtle to begin with and more obvious with each subsequent question.

This isn't to say that they should be too subtle in the first instance as you should still make bold choices, but be careful about giving the game away too early.

Pro Tip #2: If you are the Guessing Player you can ask leading questions that connect to the quirk of a Dating Contestant if you feel you have worked out what their quirk may be.

The audience will be looking to see if you have figured any of the quirks out and asking a leading question that demonstrates that you have figured things out will get a positive reaction.

For example, if you were the Guessing Player and one of the Dating Contestants was a retired boxer you could ask *'would you take me on a knockout date?'* and this would make it obvious you had figured out they were a boxer.

111: PRESS CONFERENCE

Emcee Intro Script: Our next game is Press Conference! In this game one of the players will be assigned as the Speaker at a press conference. They will be holding this press conference for an unusual and elaborate reason.

They will then have to answer questions from the rest of the cast, who will be playing Reporters.

Here's the thing...the Speaker at the press conference will not know the reason why they are holding the press conference because we will decide this whilst they are out of the room! Despite this, they will still have to do their best to answer questions. At the end they can guess to see if they know what their press conference was all about.

Challenge Style: Guessing Game

Players: 2+

Ask the Audience For: A reason to hold a press conference. I would suggest you make the reason very specific and have several details to give the Speaker more to figure out.

How to Play the Game:

#1: The Speaker should be excused from the room, or made to wear headphones so they cannot hear the audience suggestions of what their press conference will be about.

#2: Once you have the reason for the press conference decided upon, indicate that the Speaker can come back to stage/remove the headphones.

#3: The Speaker should confidently hold court and take questions from the Reporters as if they completely understand the context of every question.

#4: The Reporters should ask questions which give clues to the reason the press conference is being held, but not directly say.

As a rule of thumb, the questions the Reporters ask should avoid including any of the audience suggested words. Doing so will give away things the Speaker is supposed to guess and make it mean less when they guess correctly.

How Does the Game End?

The game ends either when the Speaker has clearly worked out the reason for the press conference, or that the Emcee feels that they haven't figured it out and that it is time to move on.

Either way, the Emcee should ask the Speaker to guess why they are holding the press conference to check if it is accurate or not.

Pro Tips:

Pro Tip #1: The Reporters could introduce themselves as journalists representing real or fictional newspapers, magazines, TV or radio stations, podcasts and such like. This will add an extra layer of realism to the proceedings and also give these players opportunities to invent amusing or ironic publications.

Pro Tip #2: There is always the risk that audience members may attempt to ask questions themselves or call out the answer. It may be worth asking the audience to not shout anything out as it will spoil the game.

In the event that the audience do say anything I would recommend that the Speaker/Guessing Player try to ignore the audience as if they haven't heard.

I would also recommend that unless it is towards the end of the game that you don't encourage the audience to ask questions.

Asking questions that give hints, but don't give away the answer is a skill that takes time to develop and, in all likeliness, you can't trust that an audience member won't say the answer by being too obvious.

112: WINK MURDERER

Emcee Intro Script: Some people think that improv is child's play, and others think it can be murder. With this next game, they're both right.

We're going to play Wink Murderer, and is a game based on the popular children's game Wink Murder. We'll have a Detective and a Murderer who will have a scene unfold around them. The Murderer is tasked with winking at other characters *(but not the detective)* and whoever they wink at dies after five seconds. The Detective will have to guess who the Murderer is before everyone else is killed. If the Detective guesses wrong, the person they guessed immediately dies.

Challenge Style: Scene based

Players: 6+

Setup: One player will need to be allocated as the Detective, and then either face away or leave the room whilst the Murderer is selected.

You then have the option whether you let all the other players, and the audience know who the Murderer is, or you can keep this a mystery. If you wish to keep it a mystery, I would suggest having the players line up and the Emcee walk behind them and tap the one selected as the Murderer on the back.

Ask the Audience For: A setting for this murder mystery

How to Play the Game:

#1: When the Detective returns to the room, the other characters should start creating a scene. I would suggest making the scene quite active and find reasons for the characters to change their positions on stage fairly regularly. This is so that it will be less obvious when a murder happens.

#2: When the Murderer is ready, they should wink at an intended victim, who should then silently count to five before performing a dramatic death sequence.

#3: This should get the attention of everyone who will react to it and give reason for the Detective to start going about the stage and questioning the various characters as suspects.

#4: The Murderer should continue to pick off victims whilst the Detective tries to work out who is doing it. I'd suggest that whoever the Murderer is, that they don't do more than one murder every minute or the game will end very quickly.

#5: The Detective can accuse someone and take a guess at who the Murderer is. If they guess correctly, it is the rule that the Murderer must confess that the Detective is right. This will take away any uncertainty, as it would be expected for a character to deny if they were the Murderer even if they were.

How Does the Game End?

When either the Murderer has been caught by the Detective, or the Murderer has killed all the other players in the game.

Pro Tips:

Pro Tip #1: Remember that the game is between the Murderer and the Detective. The other characters should not attempt to give away who the Murderer is even if they know. If anything, they should attempt to help maintain the secret even if it means they will eventually be killed by the Murderer.

Pro Tip #2: Even though the goal of the Detective is to work out who the Murderer is, don't lose sight that the main goal of the game is to create an entertaining scene.

As such, I would suggest the Detective avoid guessing who the Murderer is too quickly, even if they think they definitely know. Of course, if the Murderer does a sloppy job of hiding who they are and is blatantly seen and caught by the Detective, they should just guess so that the audience doesn't suspect the game is rigged.

SECTION 15: QUICK FIRE/JOKE TELLING GAMES

These are games which are either all about making up jokes on the spot, or coming in with quick fire responses and are good for lots of players.

I wanted to tell a joke about dynamite, but it totally blew up in my face

113: DOCTOR DOCTOR

Emcee Intro Script: It's time for a joke telling game! This round is called Doctor Doctor and is just the medicine I think we all need. The players will make up jokes that follow this rhythm:

Doctor Doctor, I feel like a blank. And then they'll make up their punch line. They'll replace the word *'blank'* with a profession, animal, object or whatever random idea you tell us.

Challenge Style: Joke telling/Quick fire

Players: 1+

Ask the Audience For: A profession, object, animal or other random element they think would finish the sentence *'Doctor Doctor I feel like a...'*

How to Play the Game:

#1: Players step forward from a line across the stage and say their version of the joke.

#2: This game follows the formula of *'audience suggestion plus the theme of doctors equals punchline'*. For example, if the suggestion was *'playing cards'* you could get jokes such as:

Doctor doctor, I feel like playing cards. Ever since I took those steroids you gave me, I feel Jacked!

Doctor doctor, I feel like playing cards. I've run out of contraception and now I've got a full house.

How Does the Game End?

Once the Emcee feels the audience have had their fill of the joke round.

Pro Tips:

Pro Tip #1: You'll want to think of terms that relate to the audience's suggestion. Then look for opportunities for how these terms could link to the idea of things you'd associate with doctors or hospitals.

Still using playing cards as the example suggestion, your thought process could be to think of any card related words or terms such as *Ace, Pack, Deck, Gin, Chips, Poker*...and think what opportunities there are to connect these to doctor related terms.

Gin is a card game, but it is also an alcoholic drink. Someone could visit a doctor to discuss not drinking anymore.

Poker is another card game, but obviously also sounds like the term to poke or *'poke her'*. You could connect this to having an injection.

In this instance you could end up with a joke such as the following:

Doctor, doctor, my wife feels like a playing card. She needs her injection...will you poke her.

114: STOPPED BY THE COPPER

Emcee Intro Script: Have you ever been stopped by a copper? That is the theme for our next joke telling game. Our performers will make up jokes that will follow the rhythm, *'why was the blank Stopped by the Copper?'* And then they'll make up the punchline.

Challenge Style: Joke telling/Quick fire

Players: 1+

Ask the Audience For: Professions, animals, objects or other words to describe things that may be stopped by the copper.

How to Play the Game:

#1: Players take turns to step forward and say their versions of the joke based on the audience suggestion.

#2: The theme of this game is police officer crossed over with whatever the audience suggestion is.

The game particularly lends itself to the Emcee getting suggestions of professions. You can then think of any crimes that someone from that profession may be likely to commit. You can also think of any crimes that may connect to the characteristics of the job. Here's some examples:

Teacher: *Why was the teacher stopped by the copper? For breaking out of the 'detention' centre.*

Photographer: *Why was the photographer stopped by the copper? For taking shots.*

Beautician: *Why was the beautician stopped by the copper? Fraud. They 'make up' things that aren't true.*

How Does the Game End?

Once the performers have done several jokes on a few different topics.

Pro Tips:

Pro Tip #1: With joke telling games such as Stopped by the Copper, look for opportunities to build off previous player's jokes. If someone says a joke where you can extend or combine ideas, the audience will usually appreciate call backs like this. Here is an example that could be told in the round about beauticians but call back to the round about photographers:

Why was the beautician stopped by the copper? Fraud. They 'make up' lies about the photographer taking shots at them.

Did you hear about the lobster mobster boss? Now he sleeps with the fishes

115: PUNVERSATION

Emcee Intro Script: It's time to play Punversation! Two characters are going to have a rapid back and forth conversation on a set theme where each line of dialogue they say must include a pun.

If I *(the Emcee)* think a performer is hesitating without a pun, I'll give them a very fast five count to come up with one and then call *'skip'*. The Punversation will then swap to the other player's turn. Whoever I judge has come up with the most puns after sixty seconds wins.

Challenge Style: Quick fire/scene based

Players: 2

Ask the Audience For: A theme for the conversation. This can be a random word such as a place, an object, or an activity.

If something is too specific, such as *a trombone,* the Emcee can interpret this as *instruments* or at least *brass band instruments*.

How to Play the Game:

#1: Players should loosely face each other and have a back and forth conversation.

#2: The aim is to include a pun based about the audience suggested theme in each line of dialogue. Each line should be one or two sentences long at most.

#3: The Emcee should award a point every time a player includes a pun. To acknowledge this has been done successfully, the Emcee should announce *'point'*. After this is announced, it will swap to be the other player's turn.

#4: If a player starts a line, but they can't think of a pun, that player can call *'skip'* to show that they are returning control of the game to the other player. This may feel as if you are giving a point away if the other player has got a pun, but it will save time that will give you more chance at scoring points later.

#5: If the Emcee thinks you are unable to generate a pun within a sentence or two, the Emcee should rapidly start a countdown.

As not to talk over the players, this countdown should be done visually by holding up five fingers and lowering them until they are all gone. If the player hasn't said a pun during this countdown, at this point the Emcee should call *'skip'* to swap back to the other player's turn.

To be clear, this is not a five second countdown but instead is as quickly as you can go from five fingers to four fingers, to three, to two, to one finger and then none.

#6: Players should avoid interjecting and talking over their opponent. The game only swaps between players when the Emcee calls *'point'* or *'skip'*, or a player calls *'skip'* on themselves.

How Does the Game End?

At the end of sixty seconds. The Emcee should then announce who managed to get the most points.

Pro Tips:

Pro Tip #1: Try to connect each line that is said to the previous line said by the other player. This will make it seem more like a conversation, rather than just random puns said one after another.

Here's an example, if the theme was instruments.

Player 1: *I have a trombone to pick with you.*

Player 2: *Really? Is it because I trumpeted how much better I am than you?*

Player 1: *No, it's because you coughed and gave me the flute.*

Player 2: *Ha Monica gave me the flu first...*

Pro Tip #2: If you can't think of a pun, try to stay in character, but it's also ok to show panic and acknowledge that you haven't got a pun. The Emcee will quickly call *'skip'* and send the control of the round back to the other player.

116: MONOPOLISED PUNVERSATION

Emcee Intro Script: We're now going to play Monopolised Punversation. In it, two players are going to have a pun filled conversation, but with capture the flag rules. Let me explain.

Two performers are going to face each other and have a rapid back and forth conversation on a set theme that will last one minute.

One player will start the conversation and have to say as many puns as they can on the theme. They will aim to do this continuously until either the time runs out, or they seem to hesitate in their flow of punning.

If the puns dry up, the other player will take over until either they mess up, or the timer ends.

Whoever has achieved the most puns on the topic within the time limit wins.

Challenge Style: Quick fire

Players: 2

Ask the Audience For: A theme for the conversation.

How to Play the Game:

#1: Players face each other and have a conversation.

#2: The Emcee will decide which player will start, as they arguably have an advantage in the game. Coin toss, alphabetically or random choice are all ok.

#3: Unlike the regular version of Punversation, this game isn't strictly turn take. Whoever starts the conversation will be tasked with continuously coming up with pun after pun in quick succession until they run dry.

The Emcee will be judging if each player is able to keep coming up with more, but if a player is unable to come up with another within a very fast five count *(this should be demonstrated with fingers on the judge's hand and not said out loud)* the Emcee should call skip.

#4: If the player says a pun that has already been said, the Emcee should call skip.

#5: If the Emcee calls *'skip'*, the other player gains control of the round and it will be their turn to keep making up puns until either the round ends or they dry up.

How Does the Game End?

At the end of sixty seconds. The Emcee should then announce which player was able to come up with the most puns.

Pro Tips:

Pro Tip #1: Don't just say random puns. Try to build a story within your scene and make the other player's presence important. Are you just telling them a story, or are you saying things expecting them to respond?

If you are the player who isn't in control of the round, still be in character and engage and show you are listening.

Pro Tip #2: If you start second, or it is the other player's turn, use this time to quickly come up with ideas and bank them. Even if the other player is in control of the round, the advantage you have is thinking time.

117: SEX WITH ME

Note: This is a game which I would only recommend playing to an adult only audience, and not at a family orientated improv show.

Emcee Intro Script: It's time to get personal. It's time to share as we play the game Sex with Me. In this game we will take suggestions of what sex with our performers may be like. They will then give examples of why sex with them is like the suggestion.

Challenge Style: Quick fire/Joke telling

Players: 1+

Ask the Audience For: Suggestions of how to finish the phrase *'Sex with me is like...'*

The suggestions you're looking for here could be anything really, but professions *(fireman, taxidermist, bus driver)* or objects *(car, table, some money)* usually work best.

How to Play the Game:

#1: The players should stand in a line or huddle. Once the Emcee has got a suggestion from the audience, the players take turns to step forward and say their version of the joke.

#2: The jokes will all follow the rhythm of saying the setup line and then the punchline. For the following example, we'll use a football:

Sex with me is like a football...most of the time it happens when I'm looking at the net.

#3: The idea of the punchlines is to draw a comparison between the suggestion and having sex. There are several different ways to approach this. These include:

Innuendo based humour where you use terms related to the audience's suggestion to also sound like descriptions of sex. Such as:

Sex with me is like a football...for best results you have to pump it up.

Humour which is based on commentary of the person telling the joke. Such as:

Sex with me is like a football...Sometimes you score and sometimes you don't...

In this instance, the person telling the joke should deliver it with a sense of disappointment as the joke is self-deprecating.

Or it can be more direct such as:

Sex with me is like football...just like sex with me, most women don't like football.

This joke is still self-deprecating but isn't based on wordplay like in the previous jokes and is a more direct comparison.

   #4: Every so often, the Emcee should get a new suggestion from the audience.

How Does the Game End?

The Emcee ends the game at their discretion.

Pro Tips:

Pro Tip #1: As the game is themed around sex, feel free to say the jokes in a more seductive tone.

Pro Tip #2: You can also play with your physicality to be more sexy or suggestive. I would only recommend this ever be playful and never too explicit or direct. A sexy walk forward, biting your lip and maybe lightly caressing your sides and hips is usually more than enough for people to get the idea.

118: LIFE WITH ME

Emcee Intro Script: Our performers are now going to tell jokes that will follow the rhythm of *'Life with Me is like a blank'* and then come up with the punch line. They'll replace the word *blank* with a suggestion of your choice and then come up with an appropriate punch line.

Challenge Style: Joke telling/Quick fire

Players: 1+

Note: This is a family friendly version of the game Sex with Me.

Ask the Audience For: Random things that could finish the sentence *'Life with me is like a...'* These could be household objects, professions, well known characters or anything else really.

How to Play the Game:

#1: Players stand in a line and once they have the suggestion from the audience, they take turns to step forward and say their version of the joke.

#2: The jokes follow the rhythm as follows. For this example, we'll use a sheep.

Life with me is like a sheep...empty without ewe

Life with me is like a sheep...I'm baaaaaa-ed from most pubs.

#3: The idea of the jokes being told in this game is to provide commentary both on the player telling the joke, but also what a relationship with the joke teller would be like. This can extend to romantic relationships, work relationships, and family relationships, such as those with your parents and children.

How Does the Game End?

When the Emcee judges that either enough jokes have been told to fill the time allotted for the game, or that the players have run out of steam.

Pro Tips:

Pro Tip #1: It's easy to lean heavily into jokes that are self-deprecating, but feel free to do the opposite and have fun making boastful claims of how good life with you would be. You'll have to judge where the fine line is between being boastful and arrogant, but you can have fun playing a confident persona.

Pro Tip #2: Building off the last tip, have the awareness of what approach others in the game are doing. If everyone is being self-deprecating, you can change things up by being confident, arrogant, or humble. You could just go one route with all of your jokes, or you could have a variety of emotions in your delivery of the jokes.

Pro Tip #3: A good rule of thumb with any of the joke telling games in this, or other Extreme Improv game books is to tell the full joke every time. This includes the full setup, the audience suggestion and then your punchline. Doing this will both make sure the audience's full attention is turned to you and also help your fellow players by giving them an extra second or two to formulate their next joke.

These games can quickly peter out and feel awkward if there are long pauses between people taking their turns. Not rushing your jokes will help the game continuously flow with fewer gaps.

119: FORBIDDEN LINES

Emcee Intro Script: We're now going to play Forbidden Lines. In this game, we'll ask the audience for suggestions of famous movies, and then take turns to step forward and deliver lines that were *'cut'* from these films.

Challenge Style: Quick fire

Players: 1+

Ask the Audience For: Famous movies

How to Play the Game:

#1: Players should stand in a line and wait for a movie to be called out from the audience or Emcee.

#2: The players should then step forward and deliver their lines which were cut from these films. Of course, these aren't going to be real lines that were cut from the films. Instead they should be made up lines that the audience will instantly understand why they were cut.

#3: Film knowledge is key for this game, so make sure the Emcee only takes well known movies that most people in the room *(on stage and in the audience)* are likely to know.

How Does the Game End?

Once the Emcee thinks the cast/audience have had enough.

Pro Tips:

Pro Tip #1: Players can either step forward alone or bring another player forwards with them to deliver the line to.

If you do this, be careful not to have too much back and forth of dialogue, as the game isn't about creating whole scenes that were cut from movies, and is specifically about individual lines.

Of course, there are exceptions to this rule, and will be times when it is acceptable to have two players exchange dialogue. For example, if you wish to parody famous lines that are only recognisable when said between two characters.

Pro Tip #2: The Emcee should mix things up and change the suggestion being used for this game after every three or four times a performer has stepped forward.

Unlike other quick fire games where I would suggest mixing things up after ten or more jokes, film knowledge is more niche and specific. Audiences and performers are less likely to have as much in depth knowledge about film references for any particular movie.

You've heard of stand up? Well, this is sit down comedy

120: HEADLINES

Emcee Intro Script: We're now going to play Headlines! For this game we've grabbed some of the biggest news headlines from today's newspapers, social media and articles online. We'll read them out, but we're going to replace at least one of the words from the headlines with the word *'blank'*. Our performers will then step forward and give their ideas of what the full headline is by filling in the blanks.

Challenge Style: Quick fire

Players: 1+

Ask the Audience For: N/A.

Setup: This game doesn't use audience suggestions. Instead, the Emcee should have a few prepared headlines

If you have a projector in which you can show the headlines this will enhance the experience for the players.

I would suggest showing each headline twice. Firstly, by showing a censored version of the headline with a word blanked out. Then secondly by showing the full headline after the players have finished guessing.

How to Play the Game:

#1: The Emcee reads out a current news headline but says *'blank'* instead of an important word/phrase.

For example, the headline could be something like:

"King Charles caught BLANK today at castle"

The original may be *"King Charles caught flu today at castle"*

#2: Performers then step forward and give their suggestions for what they think fills in the blank. I would suggest that the performers say the whole line rather than just their idea for the missing word *(although this is optional).*

Examples of ways that they could interpret this headline could be:

"King Charles caught thieves today at castle"

"King Charles caught with mistress today at castle"

How Does the Game End?

Once the performers have played through all the pre-selected headlines.

Pro Tips:

Pro Tip #1: You can replace the blank word with more than one word if it's required to make the joke make sense. As given in our example joke, *'caught with mistress'* is more words than *'caught flu'* but works as a joke.

Pro Tip #2: If you need to say a sentence or two before/after your version of the headline to add context to make your joke work this is also acceptable. For example:

'This story is about King Charles' secret past as a ninja and is King Charles caught thieves today at castle.'

121: BACK IN SCHOOL

Emcee Intro Script: Let's get nostalgic! It's time to remember the good old days when we were Back in School. This is a joke telling game where players will explain why they had peculiar and unlikely nicknames that you suggest.

Challenge Style: Joke telling

Players: 1+

Ask the Audience For: Nicknames someone may have had whilst at school. These can be things that may sound like actual nicknames, or they can be random words, names or objects.

How to Play the Game:

#1: Players stand in a line and step forward to say their version of the joke.

#2: The jokes will all follow this rhythm: *Back in school, they called me blank...*This will be followed by your punchline.

Here are some examples if the suggestion was *'Cupcake'*

Back in school they called me cupcake because I was always baked.

Back in school they called me cupcake because I was always sweet.

Back in school they called me cupcake because I was bad for your teeth (mimes punching)

#3: The jokes in this game should be a combination of things that link to the audience suggestion, combined to the theme of schools.

Things that relate to school life that you could work with include teachers, principals, gym class, French lessons, science, math, playground etc...

How Does the Game End?

When the Emcee feels you've come up with enough jokes.

Pro Tips:

Pro Tip #1: If more than one player goes to step forward at the same time, you should aim to defer to the other player to quickly negotiate who is going next. Avoid both going to speak at the same time.

Pro Tip #2: The jokes in this game can link to the idea of yourself as a young person. You can play into what you feel the audience know about you or would expect of you as a person.

This said, you don't have to make the jokes literally personal. The personal connection is something you can just choose to lean into if it helps make the joke work. You could also deliver your line in a different accent or tone of voice to denote a different character that is obviously different from you as a person.

122: MACWORTHY

Note: This game is inspired by comedian Jeff Foxworthy's *'you might be a redneck'* jokes. In Extreme Improv we were introduced to the game by a performer in our team called Jimmy Mac, who has since sadly passed away. As he was a big fan of this game, we started referring to the game as Macworthy when played on Extreme Improv shows.

Emcee Intro Script: I have nothing to promote right now, so I'll leave you with this...Our next game is Macworthy! This is a joke telling game where we'll explain why certain behaviours indicate what profession you have or type of person you are. For example: *If you always arrive at work at tooth hurty...you might be a dentist!*

Challenge Style: Joke telling

Players: 1+

Ask the Audience For: Suggestions of professions, types of people, things people may be fans of, nationalities, or even objects.

How to Play the Game:

#1: Players stand on a backline and step forwards to tell their jokes.

#2: Unlike many of the joke telling games in this book, the rhythm of the jokes in this game is slightly unusual. This is because the punchline happens in the middle of the joke and not the ending...but you'll still get a laugh at the end. I know this sounds confusing, so let's break it down.

Using the dentist joke, in most other joke telling games, the *'tooth hurty' (to sound like 2.30am/pm)* part of the joke would normally be the last thing said to end the joke.

For example, *Doctor, Doctor, I feel like a dentist...I always wake up at tooth hurty. Or, a dentist walks into a bar and the bartender says we don't open until tooth hurty.*

In this game the structure dictates that you'd say something to the effect of *'if you always wake up at tooth hurty…you might be a dentist.'*

To break it down further, I'll highlight the parts of the joke that will always stay the same in capital letters. These words won't change no matter what the audience suggestion is, or what your punchline is.

IF YOU blah, blah blah, YOU MIGHT BE A audience suggestion.

The *'blah blah blah'* will be some action or behaviour that you link to the audience suggestion and is the punchline.

How Does the Game End?

When the Emcee decides enough jokes have been told.

Pro Tips:

Pro Tip #1: If done well, you'll get a laugh at both the middle of the joke and the end. This works on the principal that the audience catch on to the rhythm of how the jokes are structured.

For example, *'if you have two pet canines…you might be a dentist'*

Because my other example jokes are based on dentists you probably could anticipate that the ending was going to be *'you might be a dentist.'* As long as the audience know what the current suggestion is, you should get a laugh in the middle, and then another at the end.

Pro Tip #2: The way you say the ending part of the joke can be varied to good effect. As the ending will be said over and over, you could build the emphasis on it to make your delivery increasingly heightened. Then when this becomes predictable, you could say it in a much more self-assured, or humble way.

Pro Tip #3: You could show a certain feeling or attitude about the profession you are making a joke about.

You could even tweak the expected ending to heighten this. For example: *If you are likely to bust a cap (both meaning break a tooth and fire a pistol)…you might be a dangerous dentist.*

123: PUN PANIC

Emcee Intro Script: Pun Panic! Each performer will be given one minute to speak a stream of conscience monologue where they have to include as many puns as possible about a topic you decide. Whoever manages to come up with the most puns wins!

Challenge Style: Joke telling

Players: 1+

Ask the Audience For: Themes/topics for the puns. This shouldn't be too specific like types of *cutleries*, so if you get something that specific, I would recommend broadening it out to *'things you keep in the kitchen'*.

How to Play the Game:

#1: One player at a time is given one minute *(which should be timed)* to keep speaking and include as many puns as they can think of on the given topic/theme.

#2: Each player will get their own topic, as it'd be too difficult for multiple players to keep coming up with puns on the same topic.

#3: The idea isn't to tell structured jokes like others featured in this book, but just to slip puns into your continuous speech. So, if the topic was cutlery or things you'd find in the kitchen, you could say something like the following:

I've got a lot on my plate right now. I'll tell you now be-fork I fork-get. But I won't say it all at once. I'll spoon feed you a bit at a time. I was spooning with my wife and telling her about when I was an eligible spatula. I ladle the facts out on the table, and also my wife is quite dishy. She'll bowl you over...

As you can see the above example doesn't tell a rich story but is an example of how you could keep talking and squeeze in more and more references to things you'd find in a kitchen.

#4: As the player is telling jokes, another person *(usually the Emcee)* will keep track of how many puns they have managed to include. This can be shown on their fingers or with a more elaborate or electronic scoreboard.

How Does the Game End?

At the end of one minute. If multiple players are taking turns, whoever achieved the most puns will be announced as the winner.

Pro Tips:

Pro Tip #1: If you are keeping score, try to judge what puns get a laugh, and award points where they managed to make a pun on the topic. You could give a point if they get a laugh outside of making puns or off topic, but this is at your discretion.

Pro Tip #2: The Emcee doesn't have to take the first suggestion given if it doesn't feel like there is much potential in the topic. If an audience member says something that isn't really a viable suggestion, such as *16th century French poets*, or *pull rings* or *Scrabble*...it may be that the audience haven't really understood what is needed in terms of a theme. If you can reshape their suggestion into something useable, like Scrabble becoming board games, then great. If not, then just clarify what you mean by a theme/topic.

Pro Tip #3: If you are playing the game, just keep talking as you try to think about your next pun. If you can't think of puns, just tell the audience you can't think of any. The game is called Pun Panic, and the more you add to the sense that you're scrambling to think of puns, the bigger the laugh/cheer will be when you hit one.

Pro Tip #4: If you go silent, it may project awkwardness to the audience. In which case, once again, I'd suggest to keep talking about things that relate to the topic you've been given.

Pro Tip #5: If you're really stuck, you could look to other players or even the audience to offer help and if they say any, you could take their puns as if you came up with them. I would say to try to avoid doing this as it'll be a safety blanket which could mentally stall you from coming up with any more yourself...but it is an option.

124: WORDS OF WISDOM

Emcee Intro Script: It's now time for some Words of Wisdom. For this game we will ask for suggestions of fictional characters, historical figures, even professions. Then our performers will step forward to and give examples of some advice, morals and general words of wisdom that is befitting of these characters.

Challenge Style: Quick fire

Players: 1+

Ask the Audience For: Suggestions of fictional characters, people from history or professions.

How to Play the Game:

#1: All players stand in a line.

#2: When you have a suggestion of a character, the players take turns to step forward and give examples of words of wisdom that the character may give. The aim here is that the advice will be something that the audience will recognise about the suggested character.

Here are a few examples of words of wisdom based on character types you may get asked to do:

Donald Duck: *If you're picking things up, remember to bend your knees. First you bend that knee, and then you bend dis-ney.*

Henry VIII: *If the barman doesn't pull a good pint, tell him it must be off with the head.*

A butcher: *Never leave people waiting. Be on time. Chop chop.*

How Does the Game End?

Once the players have each had a few turns to give some words of wisdom.

Pro Tips:

Pro Tip #1: The advice you can give as the characters can be either simple honest advice, or it can be ironic.

Pro Tip #2: What you say can be pun based, or it can be based around things you know about the character. For example:

Marty McFly *(from Back to the Future): If you're ever going to break up your parents' marriage, make sure you do it after you are born. Never before.*

These words of wisdom are a catastrophe. I'm not feline good about them

125: WHY DID YOU…

Emcee Intro Script: Audience, it's time to get to know us a little better. This game is for all of the performers and is called 'Why did you?'.

We'll ask you *(the audience)* to finish the sentence *'why did you…'* Then the performers will step forward and explain why they did what you asked. This could be the likes of why did you eat the last sausage roll, or why did you murder the postman. Whatever you like.

Challenge Style: Quick fire

Players: 1+

Ask the Audience For: Questions they would like to ask the performers. These can be general questions, or even specific to an individual performer. The questions should start with the phrase *'why did you'* or *'why are you'* rather than being general knowledge questions that wouldn't involve the player.

How to Play the Game:

#1: Players step forward to answer the questions one at a time.

#2: Once the audience has asked a question, the Emcee should repeat it to make sure everyone in the room has clearly heard.

#3: Answers can be shorter or longer, and can be pun based, or not. Unlike other quick fire games in this book, I'd say this one lends itself more to general funny answers or stories rather than just going for a pun. Here's a few examples:

Q: *Why did you burn the cake?*

Player 1: *I did it to start a fire so that the firemen would come out and my favourite one would have to rescue me and then we'd fall in love and get married.*

Player 2: *Because I want to ruin my little brother's birthday…*

Player 3: *Why did I burn the cake? I'm into forest fires and wanted to burn down the Black Forest...*

In the case of this last one, its more pun based as the Black Forest both sounds like the name of a geographical location and is also the name of a type of cake.

How Does the Game End?

The game ends when the Emcee feels enough questions have been answered by the players.

Pro Tips:

Pro Tip #1: The Emcee can judge if each question should only have one answer, or if there is room for more than one player answer each question.

Even if you do go for the latter, I'd lean away from everyone answering every question in order to make this game different from other quick fire games you may play.

The types of answers you get are likely to either be pun based or something that is slightly shocking or unusual. If you have multiple answers from players explaining twisted reasons they did the same thing, it'll get a bit samey.

Pro Tip #2: In contrast with my last point, you can break the chain of having twisted or negative sounding answers by answering with something self-sacrificing or sweet. This is likely to get an *'awwww'* response more than a laugh, and these too may wear thin if overdone.

126: BARGAIN BIN SUPERHEROES

Emcee Intro Script: It's time for Bargain Bin Superheroes! This is a quick fire game where we'll take suggestions of unusual superhero names. The players will then step forwards as these superheroes and explain why they are called these names.

Challenge Style: Quick fire

Players: 2+

Ask the Audience For: Random words

How to Play the Game:

#1: The Emcee asks for suggestions of words. The idea is that the players will take these words and turn it into a superhero name by adding Man, Boy, Woman, Girl etc after the name.

For example, if the audience suggested the word *'Spanner'* players could turn it into Spanner-Man, Spanner-Boy, Spanner-Woman, or Spanner-Girl. Alternatively, they could just say *'They call me The Spanner',* or any other variation that you feel works.

#2: Players stand along the back of the stage and when they have an idea, they step forward to take their turn. The players don't have to go in any set order and players can also take multiple turns per suggestion.

#3: When players step forward the rhythm of what they say should roughly follow this pattern:

"They call me *(Audience Suggestion)* Man and my special skill is...*(whatever your punchline is).*

Here's a few examples:

Player 1: *They call me Spanner-Man, and my special skill is going for the nuts!*

Player 2: *They call me the Spanner-Man, and my superhero origin story is gut wrenching!*

How Does the Game End?

The game ends after a few suggestions have been taken for use, and the Emcee judges that it is time to move onto the next game.

Pro Tips:

Pro Tip #1: Lean into whatever you know about the genre and theme of superheroes. Special powers, rescuing people, any weaknesses that the character may have, who their arch nemesis is and stuff like that.

Pro Tip #2: As well as playing a superhero, you can also decide to play the game as supervillains.

IX: AFTERWORD

And that's all we have time for today! Another fun filled adventure in the bag, but I can assure you, the adventures will continue. As I sat down to write this chapter, I tried to remember what I had written in the afterword of the first book. Looking back at it now, I discovered that I had said that I was already compiling a list of games for what would become this follow up book.

I can only apologise that it's taken this long. In the same spirit as I did last time, I'll again take this opportunity to say that I'm compiling games for the next book. Actually, all the games that will be in the next book, titled **'Extreme Improv 3 Super Book of Improv Games'** are pretty much locked down already. The same goes with book number 4. Book 5 is also a possibility at this stage, but I figure I've got a couple of years before I reach that point.

It takes a lot of work to compile these books, as you really have to break down the improv games in your mind to work out what any player would benefit from knowing to be able to play them well. Inventing new games is even harder.

Before I can try out the games with other performers, I've had to play through them in my own head dozens of times to work out how they'll work. Then work out how to explain them so that anyone can pick up the book and know how to get started with them.

I also have to work out that even if a game can be played, is it worth including? Or am I inventing games that are too much of a deep cut that only improv geeks will appreciate it, and they'd be lost on the audience? I would say I am definitely guilty of this with a few of them...but I'll let the readers and players decide that.

This book is the fourth that I have published, but I have near completed manuscripts of at least three more which are not about improv. On two of them, I have gotten as far as to write *'this is my fourth published book'*...so yeah, I'll have to change those if this one does in fact cross the finish line. Which if you're reading it, it did!

I've always enjoyed writing, and have written lots of articles, sketches and scripts for plays and films. I really hope I'm developing as a writer. Something I've learned from the process of writing these books is how much discipline it takes to see a project through from start to finish.

Certainly, I've done that lots of times with theatre and film stuff and am continually going further into the world of being a content creator... whatever that term exactly means. But I can certainly say that the process of writing books and the focus it needs to oversee projects that are on a larger scale is still something I'm working on.

Some people have the misconception that improv doesn't require a high level of planning, focus and dedication to make come together. For some, I guess it may just be about attending a rehearsal or a jam and making things up on the spot. I think for people that are more deeply involved with improv, especially if they are involved in the organisation of a group, or a festival, or are a teacher, you'll know that it requires a tremendous amount of work to create the shows and workshops.

My biggest hope with this book is that you, the reader, will have fun with the games included. I hope that you will learn a lot, and will enjoy exploring the different games covered. I also hope that the book sells a million copies, but heck, let's do things one at a time, eh?

I guess another important hope I have for the book is that it helps contribute to the growth of improv as a genre. Hopefully the insights I've included are valuable to the readers, and that the new and original games are ones that veteran improvisers can get excited about playing. I hope that this leads to more players getting involved with improv, and performers that are already involved in improv feeling reinvigorated by new challenges.

Ultimately, I just really love performing improv and being involved in this little section of the performing arts world. I hope to see it grow, and if I can help with that, it'll help ensure I'm able to continue doing more of it with others.

X: ACKNOWLEDGMENTS

Oh...I guess we're not quite done yet. It's just so hard to wrap things up...and that is something I know many an improviser will relate to.

I feel the acknowledgements section of a book is important, as it's a chance to put into print a little thanks for those who are supportive of you, and those you care about.

For my lovely girlfriend Rachel, who has joined me on stage, and been the first to hear about many of these new improv games years before anyone else, you get my first thanks. Just the other day you helped me work out what to name a game in this book, and our conversation has inspired another new game that will be in a future edition.

I'd like to thank my parents Jane and Philip, and my sisters Eve and Sarah, and my niece Sophie. You have all helped shape me to the person I am and have been there for me throughout my life.

I also want to take a moment to give dedication to family and friends who are no longer with us. There have been some painful goodbyes during the time I have been working on this book, and for now at least, I just want to say, you are each missed, and one day, we'll meet again.

And lastly, I'd like to show gratitude to everyone who has ever been supportive and positive towards Extreme Improv. To the performers, audiences, organisers, friends, and family, I say thank you. All your support has enabled Extreme Improv to continue to grow and evolve and most importantly, have fun.

So, as I have nothing else to promote right now, I'll leave you with this.

Until next time, stay safe, always stay XStreamed, and ciao for now!

Boom, and we're off the air!

Thank you to everyone who has supported Extreme Improv

David Pustansky